Continued Praise for

Living: The Power

"Even if you are already a great pickleballer and Zen master of life, read this book because you get to hang out with Mike Branon—he is not only a master in living thoughtfully and admirably, he is hilarious and his attitude alone is worth the price of the book.

"*Pickleball & the Art of Living* is a rich sampler of Branonisms, wisecracking and wise. It is a peek inside the mind and spirit of a passionate, lifelong seeker and student of life, and his relentless positivity will get to you, guaranteed. This book will help you fearlessly drill into whatever might be holding you back in life or on the court."

—Stuart Grauer, Founder, The Grauer School in Encinitas, CA; author, *Fearless Teaching*

"Fun, funny, and insightful! Mike Branon digs into the essence of why pickleball continues to grow and capture the hearts and minds of athletes young and old. An enjoyable and meaningful read, whether you play the game or not."

—Cammy MacGregor, Multiple Pickleball Gold Medalist, Women's Doubles, Singles and Mixed Doubles, Tournament of Champions and US Senior Open

"Mike artfully delivers tons of wisdom and value, without ego, and with lots of fun and irreverent humor. Neither my daughters in their twenties nor my mom and dad in their eighties play pickleball, but I'm giving them Mike's book, for sure. I admire Mike's casual genius. If you love chuckling, having your heart opened, and being inspired to be your very best self, then read this book!"

—Eric Kaufmann, author, *Four Virtues of a Leader* and *Leadership Breakdown*

"If you're looking to get more out of life and have a few laughs along the way, this book is for you. I'm a diehard tennis player but now I see why so many people enjoy pickleball. I know firsthand of Mike's dedication to helping others and giving through his charitable work. Now he has given us all a gift with *Pickleball & the Art of Living*."

—Barry LaForgia, Founder, International Relief Teams

PICKLEBALL & THE ART OF LIVING

The Power of Positive Dinking

To Janis,
Many happy days...

MIKE BRANON

Redwood Publishing, LLC

Printed in the United States of America
First Edition, 2020

Published by Redwood Publishing, LLC
Orange County, California
info@redwooddigitalpublishing.com

ISBN: 978-1-952106-69-9 (hardcover)
ISBN: 978-1-952106-70-5 (paperback)
ISBN: 978-1-952106-71-2 (ebook)

Library of Congress Control Number: 2020919535

Cover Design: Graphique Designs, LLC
Interior Design: Jose Pepito

For interior image credits please visit page 187.

Disclaimer: This book is designed to provide information and motivation to its readers. It is sold with the understanding that the author and publisher are not engaged to render any type of psychological, legal, or any other kind of professional advice. The content of each article is the sole expression and opinion of its author and is not meant to substitute for any advice from your healthcare professionals, lawyers, therapists, business advisors/partners, or personal connections.

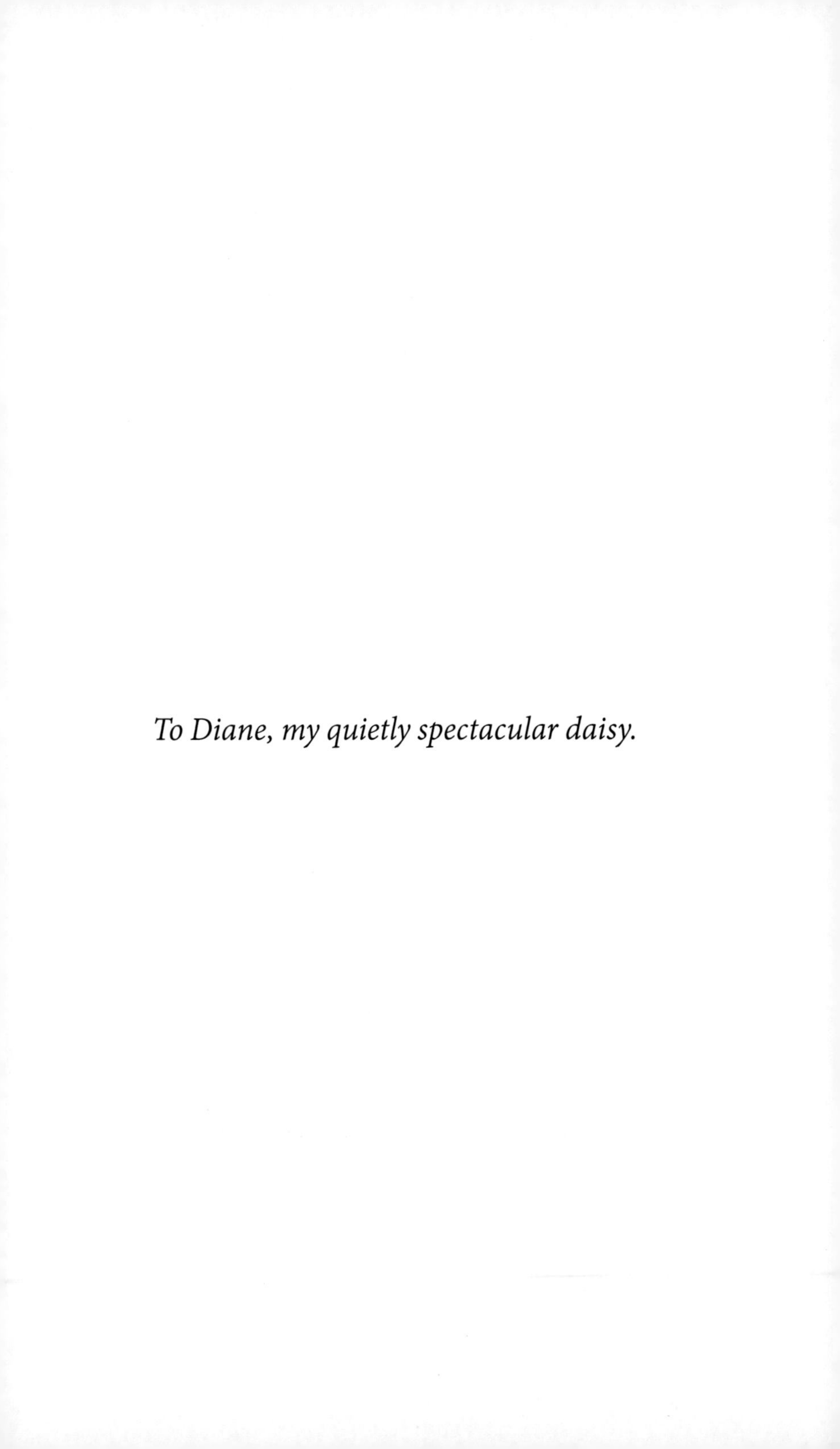

To Diane, my quietly spectacular daisy.

Contents

Foreword by Dr. Ken Druck

In my seventy-one years, I've met a handful of people like Mike Branon. In addition to being eminently wise, loving, humble, irreverent, and compassionate, this loving husband, father, friend-turned-brother, entrepreneur, philanthropist, and student of life has been wildly successful. Retired at age forty, he has traveled the world, giving generously of his time, talent, and treasure. And, as you will soon see, Mike Branon lives with his eyes and heart wide open.

The treasury of riches shared on the pages of this book comes from a special man who has faced down adversity, become an honor student in the school of life, and embodies a rare combination of honesty, humility, and authenticity. Whether you meet Mike on a pickleball court, feeding the hungry, serving on the board of a nonprofit, rebuilding homes after disasters, holding his kids and grandkids tight, meditating on a quiet hillside, or in a discussion group on Buddhist philosophy, he is the real deal. And when it comes to mastering what it really means to lead a life well lived, he is a man of great wealth.

Confident that you will find this book equally delightful and illuminating, I won't keep you for one more moment from devouring *Pickleball and the Art of Living.*

Ken Druck, PhD

Best-selling author, *The Real Rules of Life* and *Courageous Aging*

Introduction

I VIVIDLY REMEMBER SITTING ALONE ON the floor of an unfurnished room in somebody else's small house, age twenty-two, not knowing a single soul for hundreds of miles, working a dead-end job. Eight years later, there I was again, thirty years old and back in another small room in someone else's house after a divorce, financially and emotionally wounded, and needing to support a young daughter. Here I am now, age sixty, half a life later. I'm not living in a small room anymore but part of me never left those bare walls behind. I remember what it feels like to put forth good effort and seemingly go nowhere.

There are moments in our lives when we awaken to a greater awareness. My awakening took some time but once it started, it seemed to happen overnight. What was it that changed my life from frustration to fulfillment? What can you learn from my journey that has the power to lift your life to greater heights and find peace and lightness of heart along the way?

And what in the world does any of this have to do with pickleball?

Many of you love the game and enjoy the challenge, competition, and friendships it offers. Some of you are hearing about pickleball for the first time while others have heard about it but have no idea what the fuss is about. No worries. In keeping with the pickleball mantra: Everyone is welcome here!

We will explore the skills, strategies, and psychological aspects of the game, but this book is not intended to be an in-depth pickleball instructional manual. Yes, there will be ample discussion of the game in the pages to come, but the *heart* of this book is an inquiry into a life well lived, both on and off the court. In these pages, I offer a holistic approach that enables you to get the most out of your life, enjoy new friends, and have a great time.

Pickleball happens to be one of life's surprising joys for me, but anything in your life can be an enjoyable challenge. What is *your* pickleball? Is it another sport or hobby? Is it travel, music, your career, or reading great books? Is it the company of your family and friends? The art of living is an appreciation of the many aspects of life that inspire and challenge us. It is an openness to new experiences and a gratitude to be able to explore life at all.

Life isn't just a bowl of cherries or a bag of pickleballs. Many of us struggle with the push and pull of "white space" on our calendar; we feel compelled to live busy, productive lives but long for the freedom to experience life at our leisure, carving out time for reflection, relaxation, and passions like pickleball. Without a sense of balance, we swing from one extreme to the other, overcommitted and stressed or disengaged and purposeless. The end result is that we feel we never can do enough—that we never ARE enough. Self-judgment and a nagging sense of dissatisfaction can cast dark clouds over an otherwise sunny life. However, this balancing act, when brought into awareness, allows us to make peace with every stage of life. And every moment.

This book is a tribute to the pickleball community but it also explores powerful ways to get the most out of life. I want to make clear from the outset that pickleball is only a game; I'm taking poetic license in elevating it to a gateway to self-discovery. When I'm on the court I rarely am contemplating the deeper meaning of pickleball in my life—I'm trying to kick my opponents' collective butt and have a good time. But going beyond the game, pickleball serves as a relatable and entertaining example of a philosophy I hold dear: anything you do can bring greater awareness and meaning if you approach it with the right mindset.

As you may have guessed already (because you are good-looking, smart, and insightful), pickleball is a metaphor for life. Ideally, we learn how to play the game, find our strengths, work on our weaknesses, and try to win by playing hard, but playing fair. Along the way we find people who lift us up and bring out the best in us. In the end, if we learn to play the game right, we can take pride that we gave our best effort, learned from our unforced errors, and treasured the company of our fellow players and travelers.

Pickleball parables and metaphors aside, I've filled this book with the essence of what I have learned and unlearned in my sixty years. I invite you to take these insights to enrich your quest to live in harmony with others and bring the better version of yourself out to play every day.

THE ROAD MAP

None of us arrive at adulthood fully formed; we figure things out on the fly, buffeted by emotions and blown around by fate. Most of us are often too busy just getting by to pause and figure out better ways of living. And we'll never completely lose the insecurities of growing up and navigating life without a map.

If you want to be the driver of your life instead of being taken for a ride, you're going to need that map.

The map I'm offering you is this book. We're not going to speed down I-10 through Texas with eyes staring straight ahead. Think of this trip as an exploration, like poking along Route 66, A1A in Florida, or the Pacific Coast Highway, stopping at scenic lookouts and popping into quirky cafes. We will visit stops along the way to help you get the most out of your adventure. We will encounter roadblocks, find the detours, and Google Maps our way along the best routes. You will learn to navigate the world as your better self, discovering ways to maximize adventure, your backhand, and your well-being.

The goal of this journey is to fine-tune your mindset to get the most out of your game and your life—and have fun along the way.

So, let's get right to it—the motor's running. Let's look at the landmarks on your life map that can keep you headed in the right direction:

THE ROAD MAP

Assess Yourself

Before you can start the journey, you need to know where you are in the first place—be honest in your assessment. Seeing yourself clearly sets the stage for progress and fulfillment.

Develop a Growth Mindset

A growth mindset is a belief that success comes from effort, learning, and determination. Only when you believe in your power to change can you commit to the process.

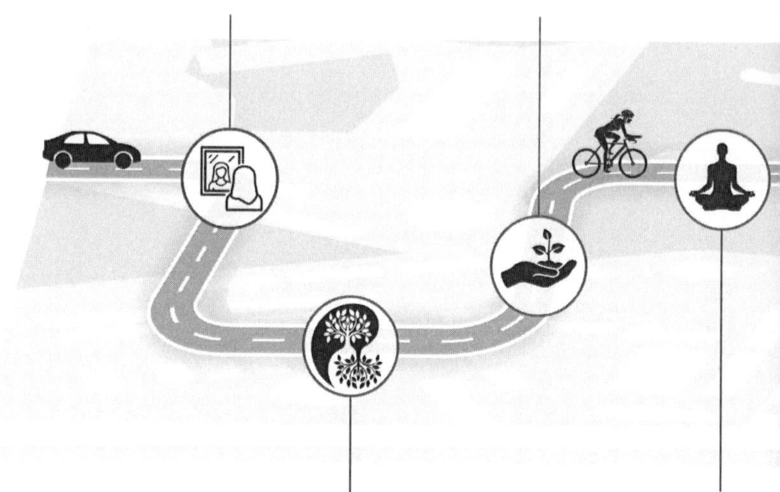

Understand the Interplay of Mind and Emotion

The unobserved mind is incapable of directing conscious change. Unobserved emotions can sabotage any rational plan. Understanding our mental and emotional selves and bringing them into unison is crucial to living well.

Engage Your Higher Self

Your body and mind truly thrive whe they are guided by wisdom principle and imbued with passion and purpos

If you follow this map, you will know where you are starting, understand where you are going, develop the right attitude and habits, and maintain the proper perspective to enjoy the journey. If you get lost at times, check back often with this road map to make sure you get where you want to go.

Create "Success Environments"

Consciously building virtuous habits provides the framework for success. Bad habits need to be replaced with new patterns that create healthy environments and yield positive results.

Live in the Present Moment

STOP! Notice life. It's amazing! We tend to get distracted—lost in thought, reliving the past and worrying about future scenarios. Be here now for that shot, that kiss, that tree, that breath... Now is the only time you truly have.

Develop Perspective and Self-Compassion

Striving without perspective can leave you dissatisfied no matter what you achieve in life. Self-compassion is the antidote to self-judgment. Try hard but accept that the destination is unknown and sometimes beyond your control. If your intentions and effort are true, you will have done your best.

WE'RE ON OUR WAY

Even with a solid road map, the meaning of life is still an intimidating subject. It has been pondered by philosophers, poets, and priests. It has been studied by scientists, scholars, and statisticians. You can get lost and confused trying to figure out what it all means. But as the guy at the local taco stand says, "You're probably better off taking a small bite than trying to down the whole enchilada at once." So let's start by asking:

What is a *day* well lived?

This is perhaps the most fundamental question we can ask. Sometimes, when we look back at our day, we know that it has been a good one. We took time to enjoy, create, and be kind to ourselves and others. The stars aligned, things went well, and we lived with a sense of purpose. And, of course, a couple of hours of pickleball with friends just took it over the top.

Then there are the times we feel like it was just another day—spinning our wheels, going through the motions, getting little if anything done. What did happen didn't add up to much. We know we're alive but on days like these, it feels like time is just drifting by.

So what sets these two very different days apart? How can we get to a place where the "good days" happen far more often than those "bad days"? It all starts with our intention as we wake up.

Each day our eyes open, our senses stir, and the endless mental conversation begins. Taking inventory of any aches and pains, the "to do" list emerges as work, family, and chores vie for priority. We might experience a swirl of emotions on the spectrum from anticipation to dread. This moment of awakening sets the stage for the day. Do we rise with excitement and a sense of purpose? Or do we awaken gray and dull, resigned to just getting stuff done and making it through the day?

Intentional living enables us to cut through the haze and chaos. To put it in sports terms, it's approaching each day with a game plan. Living intentionally puts us on the offensive rather than the defensive. We develop the habit of acting with a purpose rather than reacting to problems and losing our way. Good days start to outnumber the bad ones more often as a positive attitude frames everything in a better light no matter what actually happens.

Sure, it's a lot easier to have a good attitude when our day consists of choosing what time to get a game in on Wednesday rather than one with a stressful deadline. There will be some days when you won't feel particularly happy as things go sideways. It may seem like every one of life's shots are hitting the tape and rolling over on your side of the net as you stand by helplessly. The art of living is to accept and abide. This difficult day will pass. And it will pass with less drama and consternation if you don't expect the universe to shower you with rainbows and chocolate chip cookies every day.

Whether good or bad, or more likely somewhere in between, a day well-lived demands intention and presence. We will explore this dynamic, identifying obstacles and developing virtuous habits that enable us to play and live our best.

THE BALANCING ACT

Even when we get what we want and life is smooth, restlessness eventually creeps in. Humans evolved to wander and wonder. Is there more to life than pickleball? (I know . . . *blasphemy.*)

We complain about the challenges in our lives but without challenge, life can become shallow and tedious. Don't get me wrong, relaxation and leisure time are essential parts of a balanced life. And sharing our lives with other unique humans is part of that balance, keeping us amused, comforted, and connected. The goal is to meet life's challenges, adversities, and opportunities with optimism and equanimity, engaged and alive. The key is to find the balance that suits *you;* to use your insights and experience to consciously fine-tune your life.

Once you have examined what makes a day well lived, you just need to repeat that process day after day until you end up with a *life* well lived. Seems simple enough, right? The problem is that we are human. We are easily distracted; our minds are constantly chattering away and our emotions and desires often lead us in different directions.

Implementing the concepts in this book has reduced the distracting noise in my life and given me clarity. I have applied these principles and habits to raise a happy family, find business success, explore new life paths, become a spiritual seeker and a decent pickleball player, and enjoy all that life has to offer.

I want to offer these discoveries to you as a gift, not a lecture. I definitely don't have all the answers but have stumbled upon some clues. Please take this book in the spirit in which it is intended: a desire to make your life—and pickleball—experience the best it can be.

CHILLIN' WITH THE LAUGHING BUDDHA

Your life path is complicated. You will have questions along the way:

- How do I become more aware and build a good life in the face of hardships and heartaches?

- How do I take wise action rather than rushing around in a state of reaction?
- What does it mean to feel alive and purposeful?
- Can I actually enjoy this process and have a few laughs along the way?

These are just some of the questions that have preoccupied philosophers and seekers throughout the ages—except maybe the last one about laughter. Laughter sometimes gets cast aside in a serious search for universal truths, but as any Laughing Buddha will tell you: Enlightenment is even better when you're having a good time.

The original Laughing Buddha was a Buddhist Zen monk who lived in China more than a thousand years ago when there was no pickleball. (Can you imagine?) His name was Quieci but everyone called him "Budai." If he lived today his pals would probably call him Buddy, and he would be the one forwarding funny cat videos and doing online dance challenges. We will also call him Buddy throughout the rest of our ride because that's how he rolls when he's not at the monastery. He was devoted to the pursuit of wisdom but he loved to laugh and would remind everyone to enjoy life and be happy. Some would consider him to be out of line with the serious teachings and disciplined life of Buddhist monks but he played an important role—because what good is enlightenment if you can't share it with your pals after a game over a few beers or green teas?

Buddy loves him some pickleball.

Chances are that many of the big questions occasionally surface in *your* life but with the distractions of relationships, work, and pickleball games, these important issues are often pushed aside. This book is designed to help you focus on the essential wisdom that is the foundation for a life well lived. And then learn how to bring that wisdom into the world to create more peace and contentment in a way that is interesting, occasionally humorous, and easy to apply.

Speaking of humor, be forewarned that I have liberally sprinkled serious subjects with offbeat images and comments throughout this book. My inner Buddy just needs to get out and play sometimes. You'll get it soon enough but my message is pretty simple: Do your best, explore the wonders of life, but don't take things so seriously. After all, a life well lived should have more than its fair share of good times. When you can be mindful and ridiculous at the same time you're doing it right.

YOUR STORY, MY STORY

A FRIEND OF MINE IN THE BOOK business warned me that getting someone to read a book can be like inviting them to share an elevator with you, pushing the "STOP" button, and talking at them for ten hours. You'll probably want to get to know me better before hopping in and hoping for the best. While I hope my life story gives you some clues as to what has shaped my perspective and inspired me to share what I have learned with you, this book is really about *your* story.

Each one of us is the writer, director, and actor of our life stories. The mystery is that we don't know how it will all turn out. The challenge is to live well no matter what plot twists await us. As you read, stop and reflect on the journey you have been on and the road ahead. See if the pages to come hold any clues as to how to actively direct your life rather than let circumstances do the job for you.

Today I'm retired, living a blessed life and am married to a wonderful woman. (Despite what it seems like, I'm not married to pickleball. Pickleball and I spend a LOT of time together but I still see tennis and golf on the side.) I have two great kids and a little grandson. If you'll indulge me, I want to tell you the story of how I got here so you can better know why I am passionate about the messages I want to share.

Rowan Michael (because pictures of grandkids are always a good thing).

FAMILY: WHERE OUR STORIES BEGIN

My personal journey to finding my enough is best seen through the prism of my family. My dad was in the Navy and my mom was a nurse. Early on, they arrived at a new tour of duty in North Carolina in a Ford station wagon with $1.37 to their name. My Dad had to trade the spare tire of the car for a night in a seedy motel upon reaching Camp Lejeune.

My father is a guy you would not want to mess with. He was often embedded with the Marines in some pretty rough spots and he was known as an excellent marksman. As I got older, I heard many harrowing stories from tough military guys who knew and deferred to him; those stories would make the hair stand up on the back of your neck. But he was always a caring father to my brothers and me, spending any free time he had with us. We bounced around military bases—Key West, the Washington D.C. area, and both sides of the Panama Canal zone. Our four years in Panama were particularly memorable as we spent our time in the jungle with machetes or out on the ocean sailing and swimming with sharks and around pirate wrecks along the rugged coast.

The funny thing is, as my dad admits, my mom is probably tougher than he is. She had to raise three wolves masquerading as boys, oftentimes for long stretches by herself while my dad was away. She had plenty of practice—she grew up poor in a difficult situation where she was the caretaker of her younger siblings. She once stopped a local crime spree during our time in Panama by attacking a canoe full of bandits with her tennis racket as they attempted to scale the seawall by our living quarters. They never came back. Even now, in her eighties, I have yet to see her take more than she gives in any aspect of her life.

The Branon boys—I'm the one with my pet barracuda, Barry (circa 1972).

My younger brothers were no shrinking violets either. They grew into the size of linebackers and made their living with their hands and guile, sometimes on the wrong side of the law. My youngest brother had movie-star looks, charisma, and an appetite for power. Unfortunately, he never found his "enough" and couldn't stop even when he could afford to do so. In spite of his good qualities and his devotion to his friends and son (who was tragically murdered), he is doing life in prison. My middle brother is the only guy I know who may be as tough as my youngest brother. He is funny as hell, cares deeply for animals, but has little patience with humankind. Like my dad, he is a great ally and a terrible enemy.

There was never a lot of open affection in our family, but there was a lot of laughter and we all knew we had each other's backs. Having such tough, hard-working parents instilled a drive in me that has never completely gone away. I was the white sheep of the family. I excelled at school and loved music and sports. I couldn't bear to lose at anything and finally came to realize that I was driven in part by a desire to never let my parents down. My dad sensed this, and in spite of his success as a military officer and, later, an accomplished novelist, he took every opportunity to tell self-deprecating stories about himself. Neither he nor my mom ever put the least amount of pressure on me, knowing that there was plenty of that inside of me already.

After a successful academic career, I hit a wall in the job market, utterly failing for the first time. I made ends meet by working in a convenience store and refereeing basketball part-time. Eventually I got married and found a somewhat decent job working almost entirely on commission, but I was never really okay with just being okay. I was happy enough but was unduly hard on myself and sometimes others.

My job became less fulfilling as time went on. I had been working for a steel construction company for eight years and had plateaued as far as opportunity and challenge. My marriage was also falling apart. The only thing that kept us together was momentum and our young daughter. Divorce finally became inevitable and I found myself on my own in a small rented room in a stranger's house. I felt the sting of failure more acutely than ever. Fortunately, through trial and error, wrong turns and confusion, I eventually figured something out:

A life well lived is a celebration of who you are. It is not belittling yourself on some level for who you are not.

Sitting on the floor with my two-year-old daughter in that room, I finally had time to let that discovery sink in. The joy of just being with my daughter and seeing the curiosity and optimism in her made my entire surroundings and life situation fade into the background. I tried to put all the noise and doubt swirling around in my head aside and reacquainted myself with living in the moment, something kids do naturally. Only then was I able to rebuild my life from scratch.

Armed with this healthier mindset, I transitioned into a new relationship with someone I had known for years and who had a young son of her own. As John Madden used to say, "BOOM," instant family! I also began to look at my career and explore ways to forge my own path. I had developed ideas about what my own company might look like and established relationships that would allow me to hit the ground running. I just had to pull the trigger, but child support and a new mortgage payment left me fearful of starting from scratch with no guaranteed paycheck.

Finally, I mustered the courage to make the move. I decided to concentrate on the self-storage construction market, seeing a niche opportunity in a relatively new industry. I attacked the new venture with energy and determination and opened my own construction business in my dining room. Through hard work, good coworkers, and a lot of luck, I was on my way to a life I never knew I could have.

After six years, the company had grown to become one of the leaders in the industry. But the constant stress and time away from the kids had begun to wear on me. One day, as I was taking the train back home along the Pacific coast after another grueling week, I gazed wearily at the crashing waves and the horizon beyond. I suddenly realized that the noise I had worked so hard to push aside had found its way back into my head. I had spent the last seven years so focused on the grind that I hadn't even noticed.

That train ride home allowed me the time to reassess my journey and truly see the opportunity before me. I once had the fortitude to start my own business and now I needed to summon that same conviction to leave safe harbor and head out toward the horizon of new and uncertain possibilities. I stepped back and my staff stepped up and did fine without me. A new chapter had begun and I was excited to see how the story would unfold.

MY SECOND ACT

After I left the company, I spent the next year building my family's new home in the San Diego area. I was looking for a new challenge and building a home turned out to be the perfect transition to the next phase of my life.

I had found a level of peace and gratitude, but still felt compelled to take on new challenges that were appropriate to my state of mind. I went to massage school to learn skills that would help my aching body and enable me to help others. My wife and I traveled like never before, enjoying adventures with our kids and friends. I devoted myself to the nonprofit sector, serving on boards and working on special projects. Most importantly, I embarked on a spiritual journey that opened my eyes to new ways of seeing things. For the first time, I actively explored a world I never seemed to have time for in the past. I devoured great books and joined groups to feed the spiritual self that I had been too busy to fully examine.

It was a revelation—I was able to find new ways of being that added immeasurably to my experience of life. I was still engaged with creating and exploring, but possessed with a newfound feeling of acceptance and serenity.

As my fourth and fifth decades flew by, my kids moved out and became independent. My hair went on vacation without me and never came back. (I hope it's having fun somewhere.) Wrinkles have appeared and arthritis is knocking on the door, but I love my wife, family, and friends. I continue to learn and seek truth in a post-truth world. I play pickleball, sip my bourbon, try to savor every day and appreciate the many good people I have encountered along the way.

I have had the privilege of working with numerous charities and have traveled at home and abroad to provide rebuilding efforts after natural disasters and healthcare to those in need. I have served on the board and taught world religions and psychology at a school that values holistic education in the best sense. I have supported and overseen leadership programs for young women and bereavement counseling for those who have lost a loved one. With these programs, I've seen families moving back into their once destroyed homes, somebody's health or vision restored, and was able to hug a mother or child who had been given a new chance to cope with their own cruel luck—these are the satisfying moments when compassion meets action. I am inspired by those who do much more than me to ease suffering and bring light back into the eyes of those whose dreams have dimmed.

But this is my journey. You have a completely different life path to navigate. Your dreams will differ from mine. But at its core, your journey has the same purpose—to learn how to end up with a life well lived. I'm sharing what worked for me in the hopes it can make your pickleball and life experience more enjoyable and meaningful too.

3

PROGRESS, NOT PERFECTION

THE PURSUIT OF PERFECTION CAN BE A noble quest, but when perfection becomes an obsession, you may become blind to learning experiences and joyful moments along the way. You can be left feeling disillusioned by your inability to reach an unrealistic goal.

When you expect perfection from others, you are setting them up for failure as well. In spite of what Jerry Maguire says, "*You . . . complete me*" is a pretty hard standard to live up to. But, "*You . . . are a valued complement to me and I appreciate you for who you are as we both seek to navigate life together and as individuals. How does Mexican food sound tonight?*" probably wouldn't have been as catchy. And Renée Zellweger would have nodded off halfway through his monologue.

My unrealistic relationship with perfection had been holding me back. Getting divorced woke me up. Walking away from my business set me free. It took years to learn that trying to be perfect was a fool's game. I had to realize that divorce wasn't giving up—it was waking up to reality. The "perfect husband" image I had been trying to cultivate (and failing to reach) was holding me back from real progress in my life. And the outsized image of the successful businessman was an illusion as well; it was just part of who I was.

If I had remained a prisoner to the status quo and been afraid to change, my life wouldn't have turned out so well, and I never would have known any different.

By all means, take on the challenge of living well. But give yourself a break too. We're human, and every one of us is a work in progress. And the world we live in is unpredictable. There's no need to immediately jump ship when things aren't going as planned. By all means, stick with a good spouse or a rewarding job; they don't have to be perfect any more than you do. But don't be afraid to turn the car around when you see the "Dead End" sign in front of you.

Expecting perfection on the court is a guaranteed method for having a bad time too. Give yourself a break. And by all means, give your pickleball partner a break too. Nothing is less attractive in a partner than eye rolls, grunts of disapproval, or heavy sighs. They didn't show up to try to miss shots and ruin your day. Enjoy the process and face challenges with optimism, humility, and courage. Treasure the little victories and savor the progress you are making.

A day well lived or a game well played is one in which you have consciously given the best version of yourself, no matter what that is.

So why should you listen to me? I don't pretend to have invented a groundbreaking system that unlocks the secrets of the universe in a catchy ten-step program. I have no agenda to upsell you with my *Unleash Your Inner Pickleball Goddess* or *Pickle Your Way to a Flatter Stomach* sequels.

Am I qualified through education or profession to pontificate on the meaning of life? Um . . . no. I'm not a doctor nor do I play one on TV. As I mentioned earlier, my career and life path have taken a lot of twists and turns. I worked at McDonalds, in a factory, managed retail stores, ran my own construction company; was certified as a massage therapist, bereavement facilitator, and bartender; helped oversee nonprofits; taught high school; and co-owned a micro-brewery. And that's just a partial list of my job history. Talk about ADD . . .

However, I've also spent a lot of time reading, observing, and practicing—in other words, gathering information, seeing what works for me, and applying it to real-life situations. I hope this book will save you from the wrong turns that I have made and the time I've wasted as a result. I want to offer you a Whitman's Sampler of useful nuggets (because life is like a box of chocolates) that inspire you to find out what makes life delicious for you.

We all have different views, experiences, and opinions about what makes a good life. Ideally, we could sit down, share ideas, and figure it out together over a few beers like I do with my friends. But now, after all the time we've spent together, I feel like you and I have gotten pretty close already. You're feeling it too? Awww . . . thanks. So let's do this.

THE ROAD AHEAD

If you feel like more happiness and a more enjoyable pickleball experience might be a good thing, here's where I want to take you in the following pages:

First, we will take a look at why we play this game. If you're new to pickleball, perhaps this section will pique your curiosity and encourage you to pick up a paddle and join in the fun. And even if you're a grizzled veteran maybe you will get something out of my perspectives on the game.

Then we will explore ways to live better and achieve a greater awareness that is in alignment with your legitimate needs and desires. We will dig deep to examine the roadblocks that conspire to keep you from thriving and explore insights to inspire you to find greater meaning and contentment on and off the court. Along the way, we will discuss everything from meditation to dinking, spirituality to strategy, emotional intelligence to just having a good time. The idea is to align yourself with what is true and meaningful to you as you navigate an unpredictable world filled with crazy people like us.

Many of you have already pretty much found the life balance you want. Take any advice in the spirit it is given . . . from a desire to help. I hope you enjoy the ride. If not, I hope the size of the book is just right for sticking under one of the legs on your Christmas tree stand. That way at least I'll have contributed to a sense of balance in your life one way or the other.

You may notice that I will be speaking directly to you in the chapters to come. I don't want to deliver a lecture; I prefer a conversation. Granted, it's going to be somewhat one-sided, but if I start to drone on you can just shut the book and go for a walk. I won't mind. And your dog will be thrilled. In fact, I would prefer you read this book in small chunks and occasionally contemplate what you have read instead of steaming ahead at full speed. Part of my message is to pause and take notice, to live mindfully and become aware of the cruise control that may be taking you to destinations you don't really want to visit. In fact, throughout the book I will gently remind you to stop and consider something that has, in my opinion, earned a contemplative pause. Since I'm a dog person, I will insert a pause (paws) symbol after a thought that invites contemplation, invoking the footprint of one of my favorite dogs ever, Crash. May he always chase rabbits but refuse to hurt them.

WARNING!

There's a little bit of a self-help vibe in this book.

I have to admit that I back away a little bit when I hear the term "self-help." The genre has produced and continues to put out worthwhile information in a sincere attempt to help people live their best lives and make the world a better place. Many of these books seek to explore crucial philosophical questions in a way that makes deep truths more accessible and user-friendly. But sometimes, as the following real book titles (with my side notes) make clear, the self-help train goes off the rails.

The Beginner's Guide to Sex in the Afterlife

(Make sure to pay particular attention to the halo. It will make her wings flutter.)

Why Cats Paint

(Because they stepped in paint?)

How to Live with a Pregnant Wife

(Step 1: Don't let her see you reading this book.)

You're Sharp Enough to Be Your Own Surgeon

(Uh, no. You're not. Put down the knife.)

Natural Bust Enlargement with Total Mind Power

(Written by a man. So remember, when he's staring at your cleavage, he's just trying to help.)

How People Who Don't Know They're Dead Attach Themselves to Innocent Bystanders and What to Do About It

(Okay. That actually sounds useful.)

If any of those titles make you want to put down this book and explore something *really* interesting, I get it. Otherwise I invite you to come along and see if my twisted version of pickleball self-help is more arousing than sex in the afterlife. Besides, you'll have a lot of time for that later.

OUR YELLOW BRICK ROAD

In *The Wizard of Oz*, each of the main characters eventually comes to realize that they already had what they were searching for—a brain, a heart, courage, a home. The Yellow Brick Road is literally ***our*** life path. The wicked witch and flying monkeys (I'm still a little scarred by them) are the internal and external forces fighting to keep our heroes from finding out that their true selves were already enough. They simply had to discover what lay hidden from them.

Buddy tells me there is a Buddhist concept that we are all gems. We just need to be polished through right mind, action, and thought to let our true nature shine. So again, here is the (yellow brick) road before us . . .

I don't care much for the belief that we are innately sinful and bad in some way. This book is intended to serve as a guide to help you find your way home to the good already within you. We will travel the path together to uncover our best selves and enjoy the game we love. You will learn to deal with the flying monkeys in your brain that keep you from getting the most out of your abilities. And finally, you will learn to fine-tune your experience to achieve a balance that suits you and makes those around you happy you showed up on the court and in their lives. It really is that simple . . . and that hard.

Now let's kick some Wicked Witch butt.

CREATION

WHEN I FIRST STARTED TO WRITE THIS book, I went to the Pages app on my computer. I selected the "Blank" page option. Then I clicked "Create." A white void stared back at me, cursor blinking. My fingers hovered over the keyboard as I stared right back at the screen, facing the daunting task of creating something from nothing. I can picture God hunkered over his computer back in the day, having first created coffee and donuts in His infinite wisdom. First day on the job and He had a whole universe to create. No pressure . . . Mrs. God had been after Him for a while to do something constructive. "Honey, that universe isn't just going to create itself."

Each day we are tasked with creating our own little universe. But unlike the Big Fella, we didn't start out fully formed and omnipotent. We have only gradually become conscious on our journey from soft food and drooling on our way to the same destination. We have landed on a planet in a particular place, time, and circumstance with no operating manual and a software system with quite a few bugs in it. We are driven to distraction by our emotions and culture. We are affected by events beyond our control, compelled to survive and compete just to carve out a temporary existence. And for the final hurdle, we don't know where we're going and what it all means.

God had it easy.

How do I create my life? How do I live it well? How do I finally beat [YOUR PICKLEBALL NEMESIS HERE]? Even when we know a lot of the answers, we can still manage to effortlessly screw things up. The problem is that an often-irrational person has been given the job of carrying out a rational plan. FYI, that irrational person is you. (And me.)

RATIONALITY AND HABITS

> "The problem of human suffering is never too much rational thinking."
>
> – *Sam Harris*

To the extent we can become more rational in our approach to life, we consciously reduce suffering in ourselves and others. We realize this intellectually. The problem is that our emotions are so powerful that rationality is often pushed aside as we indulge the urgency of our desires. Rationality is often just a distant tree in our mental landscape.

I want to empower you to make positive changes and think differently about the way you experience life and your game. Take these nuggets and put them to good use. You will see the wisdom in achieving a state of mind and body that brings you fulfillment and enriches the lives of those around you. And despite my occasional joking, I sincerely want to open a discussion with you about great ideas and how to bring them into the world for the benefit of all. I hope you will find yourself nodding your head and thinking, *Yeah. That makes sense. I should do that. I'm going to start putting a plan together. Real soon.*

But . . .

But . . .

We are not rational beings. We are rationalizing beings.

How else do you explain the relationship, financial, health, political, and social decisions we make? Honestly, we usually know the right thing to do. (Yes, there *is* truth in the statement, "Trust your gut.") We just get carried away by emotions and desire. We don't pause to look carefully and logically at our decisions *before* we make them. (FYI, that is the best time.) Instead, we go through much of life unaware of the power our emotions have to sidetrack our best intentions when they are not observed. The result is we develop habits that take root in our neural pathways and lead us through life like a dog on a leash.

The key that unlocks the door to the game and life you want is building new habits that are rational *and enjoyable*. The enjoyable part is essential—this is a direct appeal to your emotions, because we resist what we don't enjoy.

The "Jedi Mind Trick" to building new habits successfully is to change your relationship with the concepts of discipline and challenge. Embrace change and feel the joy that comes when you take charge of your life rather than being swept along by the random currents of your unexamined emotions.

First, you must find your "why." ***Why is this important to me?***

Then the question becomes "how." ***How do I do it?***

And last, figure out "what" you need to be able to answer the why and the how. ***What information can I gather to make it happen?***

When you find a level of commitment and attitude that work in concert with a solid plan that makes you feel good, you are on your way.

I have found that habits beat willpower and good intentions every day of the week. So, you want to make changes in your life? Great. But it's not enough to just want—you must find a way to embed that change into a new habit. That way you don't have to think about it or motivate yourself to do it. It just gets done.

Habit and change are deeply connected in that a consciously established habit is the structure within which change happens. Willpower comes and goes—habit takes willpower out of the equation. Want to stretch and breathe deeply every morning? Schedule it like you would schedule an important conference call. Want to eat better? Make a list of foods you enjoy and that are good for you. Then bring almost nothing else into your home. Want to play your best? We know we need to get solid instruction, drill to build skill, and practice with a purpose. But if you don't schedule it (i.e., make it a habit)—it will get lost in the shuffle.

To reinforce good habits, spend some time after you stretch, eat well, or play well to savor the feeling. Give yourself a pat on the back. If you develop rational habits and practice positive reinforcement, your emotions will "call shotgun" and come along for the ride. Otherwise, they will take the wheel and drive you to distraction.

MINDSET

Dr. Carol Dweck's book, *Mindset: The New Psychology of Success,* explores the difference between two types of mindsets: fixed and growth.

- A **FIXED MINDSET** is characterized by a belief that innate ability is an unalterable trait: failure or success is seen as a judgment of one's self worth.

Therefore, failure is to be avoided at all costs as it is viewed as a condemnation rather than an opportunity to learn. Fear of failure limits opportunities to learn and undercuts perseverance.

- A **GROWTH MINDSET** is a belief that success comes from effort, learning, and determination. It holds that we are capable of changing our mindset and our lives for the better.

Protecting our image becomes less important because we recognize that we have the power to change if we take a rational approach to building new, beneficial habits. We can break free of what no longer serves us, opening ourselves to possibilities we never knew existed when we were stuck in our old ways. "Failure" is seen as a learning experience and an opportunity for self-reflection, growth, and to begin again, stronger and wiser than before.

Mindset is more important than ever in our increasingly polarized world. A fixed mindset interprets differences as threats to our very being; we live in fear of the other. We become our beliefs, unable to process facts that are contrary to our worldview because they are perceived as a denial of our identity. This can be detrimental not just to us personally but to those around us. Instead, a growth mindset allows us to be open to new information and seek to understand and find common ground. It frees us to change our opinions and value truth and common bonds rather than retreat into identity politics and tribalism. A growth mindset allows us to apply a positive approach to our sense of self as well as to interactions with the people around us.

The good news is that most of us are already somewhere on the spectrum between fixed and growth mindsets. But awareness of this dynamic is the key to consciously moving ourselves in the direction of personal growth.

Consider where you are on the mindset spectrum. Even if you have been fixed in certain ways, you have the power to transcend your conditioning and old habits. How might you benefit from a recalibration of the way you see your potential to learn and engage with life? Think in specifics. Focus on one area and check in with your self often to feel the difference it makes. A positive shift in one area can carry over into other aspects of your mindset as well.

Matthew Blom is a former pickleball champion who fulfilled his goals as a competitive player. After climbing the pickleball mountain he focused more intently on his spiritual quest. When the opportunity arises, he travels and shares what he has discovered. Blom says that 80 to 90 percent of pickleball and life success is not a matter of new or more information, but a matter of mindset. For example, many beginning and even intermediate players know they should get up to the net but fear and anxiety override their knowledge and they are hesitant to establish position and stay there.

For Matthew, self-assessment is the starting point to effectively meet the challenges you face; I couldn't agree more. It's so important to assess yourself and explore your own path to maximize your growth mindset and find ways to view your game and your life in a more positive light. Keep in mind that nurturing your growth mindset will open doors that may have been closed to you before. Your game and your life can become less stressful and more satisfying when they don't reflect your self-worth. This is at the heart of your quest: the ability to transcend self-judgment, approach your potential, and find lasting happiness.

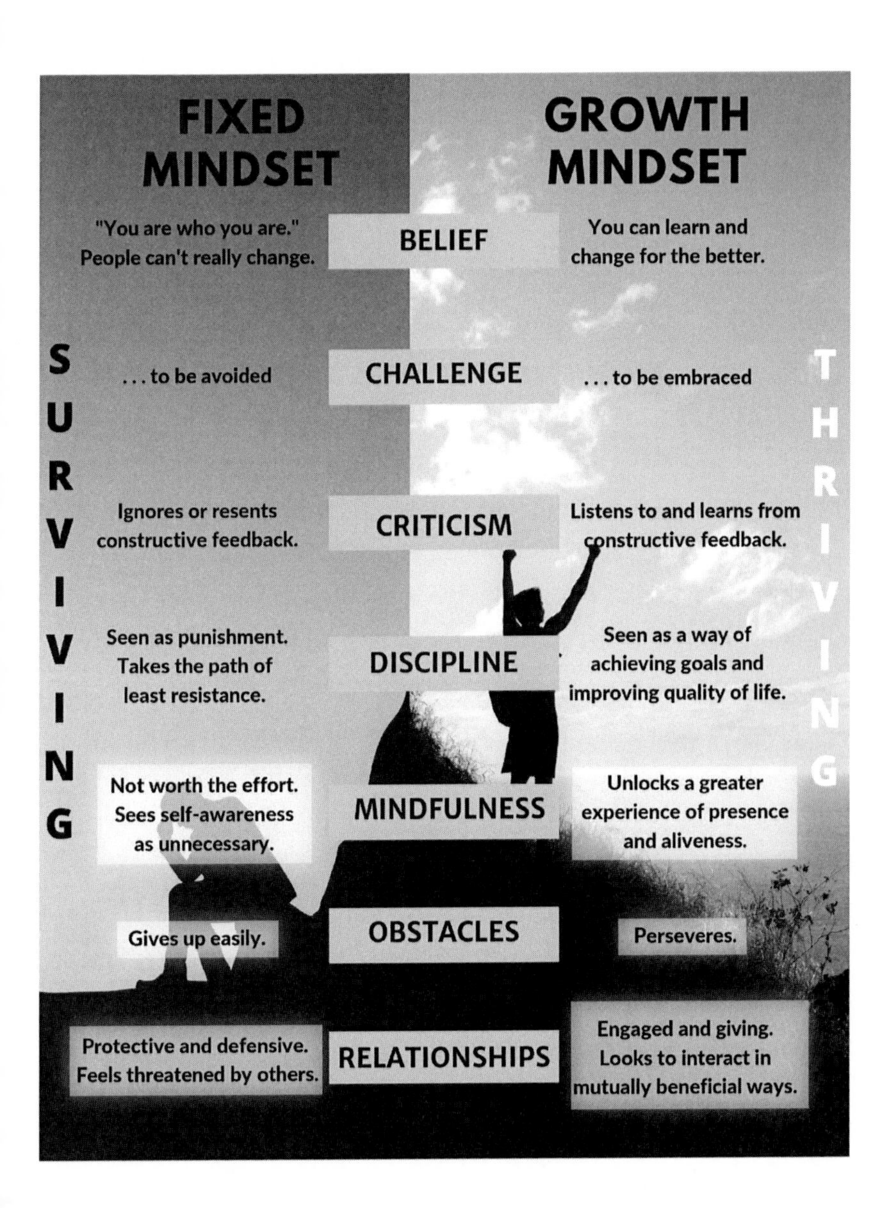
FIXED MINDSET
GROWTH MINDSET
"You are who you are." People can't really change.
BELIEF
You can learn and change for the better.
... to be avoided
CHALLENGE
... to be embraced
Ignores or resents constructive feedback.
CRITICISM
Listens to and learns from constructive feedback.
Seen as punishment. Takes the path of least resistance.
DISCIPLINE
Seen as a way of achieving goals and improving quality of life.
Not worth the effort. Sees self-awareness as unnecessary.
MINDFULNESS
Unlocks a greater experience of presence and aliveness.
Gives up easily.
OBSTACLES
Perseveres.
Protective and defensive. Feels threatened by others.
RELATIONSHIPS
Engaged and giving. Looks to interact in mutually beneficial ways.
SURVIVING
THRIVING

HARDWIRING HAPPINESS

In *Hardwiring Happiness*, Dr. Rick Hanson points out that we are hardwired through evolution to notice and dwell on the negative. In ancient times, Thog, who imagined there was danger behind every rock might have been a neurotic mess but he was probably more likely to survive than Garg, who had a delightful attitude but walked into the forest every day looking up at the sky and taking deep, cleansing breaths while being stalked by the neighborhood saber-toothed tiger. Unfortunately we are Thog's descendants, constantly obsessed with what might go wrong and possessed with brains wired to be pessimistic.

Think about how it feels when something goes wrong. Everything from disappointment to outrage can run through our minds. But do we expend the same amount of energy and devote the same focus to things that go right? Not at all. I can manage to drive my car for tens of thousands of miles, successfully avoiding all kinds of hazards. It's not even a blip on my mental radar. But when I walk out to my car in the parking lot and there's a nice door ding from somebody who opened their car door into mine and drove off, all hell breaks loose. Anger erupts. I can't wait to tell everybody how some idiot did this to my car (to me).

The news media and internet sites know very well how we are hardwired to look at the negative. They want your attention because your attention means dollar signs to them. It's no wonder that news items feature headlines designed to cater to our attraction to drama and conflict: "If it bleeds, it leads." Reality TV shows are edited to show us the most outrageous moments of bad behavior. Game highlights may omit some scoring plays but they never miss the chance to show a fight between players.

As Dr. Hanson points out, "Your brain has a negativity bias that makes it like Velcro for negative experiences and Teflon for positive ones."[1]

The only way to cope effectively with this reality is to rewire your thinking through mindful practice.

Take time to savor good experiences and revel in the gratitude you feel. In other words: Notice when things go *right*. This is an occasion to implement positive neuroplasticity and build new habits of thinking.

The pickleball court is a perfect laboratory for experimenting with hardwiring happiness. Observe how you and others react to missed shots and good shots. Which ones produce the most intense, loud reactions? Notice when you are dwelling on negative thoughts and living in the past on the court. Learn to hit the "clear history" button in your mind and come back to the current point. Give yourself credit for a smart play even if you miss the shot, and if you hit a winner, take a few seconds to appreciate the little victory before moving on. (Try to stop just short of gloating and talking trash, if possible.) If you get irritated by anyone or get mad at yourself, ask yourself how long you want to hold on to that emotion. Once you start the rewiring process you really *can* make this choice about how long you want to marinate in negativity before getting on with the reason you're here—the enjoyment of the game and your friends.

It's especially important to take some time after you're finished playing to appreciate that you are blessed to be able to play at all. Gratitude springs from those moments when you realize that most

---

[1] Rick Hanson, "Introduction," in *Hardwiring Happiness* (Random House USA, 2015), p. 2.

of the world will never get this opportunity. And some day, injury or infirmity will sideline you as well for periods of time. Eventually there will come a day when you can no longer play at all. It would be deeply gratifying to look back on your playing days and say to yourself, "That was an awesome part of my life and I got the most out of it that I could. I appreciated every moment, did my best, and enjoyed the people I met along the way."

To download the mindset infographic on page 31, visit mikebranon.com/mindset.

5

ENOUGH WITH ALL THIS STUFF, LET'S TALK ABOUT PICKLEBALL

APPARENTLY, WHEN YOU WRITE A book, editors ask pesky questions like "Why are you doing this?" and "Who is your audience?" (I didn't know there was going to be a quiz. I would have studied harder.)

The short answer to the first question is that I'm doing this for you. Don't get all misty-eyed but I really want to help you get more out of life and your game, and do it with a smile. Just remember, when you took a chance on this book you invited me in, and like your old college roommate who just "stopped by to crash for the weekend," I'm here now and might stick around for a week or so. (By the way, you're out of beer.)

The harder question is about who I am writing for (or as my picky editor would say, "for whom I am writing"). Is this a guide for a young person to get a head start and avoid a lot of the mistakes and wrong turns we oldsters have made? Am I speaking to you guys and gals in your thirties and forties who are working to support your families while trying to find enough hours in the day to find some kind of life balance? Or is this book for those of us who have somehow gotten past the "provider" stage and are dealing with issues of meaning, aging, and beating that obnoxious couple who high-five after every winning shot? (Get a room!)

The answer is yes. I'm speaking to all of you. Even if you don't play this game, you will see how approaching challenges with the right mindset can enable you to consciously shape your life. I'm also speaking to the pickleball community, people from a variety of backgrounds who share a common passion. We may skew older, but as I look around I see a younger and more diverse crowd showing up to play. We still have a little bit of a secret cult mentality. When I used to mention pickleball, 90 percent of the time people would respond with a resounding "Huh?" These days that percentage has gone way down as word has gotten out about the silly game with the funny name. Pickleball participation has increased by 650 percent over the last six years, according to the USA Pickleball Association.[1] The game is here to stay so we might as well figure out how to get the most out of it.

Pickleball is also big on cringeworthy puns. Most of these have to do with "dinking," the finesse shot played in the "kitchen" area. (Yes, we have our own language.)

---

[1] Loudin, Amanda. "Pickleball: The fastest growing sport you've never heard of." BETTER by Today (NBC News).

Dink rhymes with words like think and drink so it has spawned a plethora of dink puns that adorn the shirts of pickleball nerds everywhere:

"Dink Responsibly, Don't Get Smashed"
"I Dink, Therefore I Am"
"Great Minds Dink Alike"
"Carpe Dinkem"
"I Have a Dinking Problem"

Pickleball puns are part of the game. Just *dill* with it.

In case you haven't figured it out yet, I can be less than serious. Pickleball suits me because it doesn't take itself too seriously either. After all, consider the name. According to one of its founders, it was named after a pet dog, Pickles, who would chase the ball and run off with it when they were trying to play.

I did take some crap from my tennis and basketball friends when I told them I had started playing pickleball. I secretly wished it had been named something more macho like "Smash-Frenzy!" or "Slam-Ball!" but so it goes. The sport continues to boom in spite of the name.

The best players are bringing the game to new heights with more power and athleticism, but on some level it will always be a quirky little game played by older folks around the country who are looking to get out, knock the ball around, and have a good time. And those friends who laughed at me? They're starting to join me on the court.

PICKLEBALL (LIFE) LESSONS

I discovered pickleball a few years ago and have thoroughly enjoyed the game and the people I have met. I describe it as what might have happened if tennis and ping-pong had a one-night stand and nine months later, pickleball was born. I even teach the game part-time these days. I am always gratified to meet players who at any age have a love of learning. One of the things I focus on with them is not just the acquisition of new skills but the process of "finding you are enough."

Some people are very hard on themselves when they make mistakes. They talk to themselves out loud or internally in ways they never would speak to someone else. I point out that *mistakes are not an indictment of your character but an opportunity to see where you can improve your skills.* I also discuss the comparison trap that can leave you unhappy because of an inability to be as good as a player of a higher level. In addition I examine how to deal with other players who are critical or have a negative attitude.

These lessons apply equally well to any activity or sport. Negative self-talk, internalizing mistakes, feeling less by comparison, and dealing with difficult people are impediments to happiness. When you learn to navigate these roadblocks on the court your attitude becomes an asset. Just as in life, you are free to immerse yourself in the game, enjoy the challenge, and meet some great people.

WHY PICKLEBALL?

Many of us have competed in other sports but have found that this game in particular has gotten a hold on us. What makes pickleball so special? If you have played the game for a while, you probably have been asked a variation of that question at some point, probably accompanied by a quizzical look and some degree of skepticism. For me, the answers are varied but here are a few that may resonate with you.

Like other sports, pickleball is an opportunity to compete, develop skills, and get some exercise. What sets it apart for me is the mix of finesse and power, the unique strategy, and the accessibility to all ages and skill levels. Above all, it's a social game at heart. I occasionally close my eyes between games and listen to the (mostly) happy voices rising above the staccato "thwacks" of paddle on hard plastic. It's a cozier, more intimate vibe than tennis where there is more space between the players.

I sometimes find it hard to believe that I have been so fortunate to be able to spend part of this chapter of my life knocking a yellow, plastic ball around with a bunch of nice people. There are still stressful parts of life for all of us, but our time on the court is a blessing. Politics, pandemics, and inequality might be waiting for us when the games are over, but while we're on the court, the only thing that divides us is a net.

Morgan Evans, a pickleball pro, coach, and all-around fun guy, points out that tennis demands a level of physicality that is not as essential in pickleball. He's not a big guy but has learned how to use a variety of skills to even the playing field. He enjoys the never-ending challenge of attack, counterattack, and disguising shots as a strategy to beat more physically gifted players. There are many ways to win at pickleball; it's a puzzle that keeps us physically and mentally engaged.

Another attractive aspect of the game is that it is a perfect blend of physical and social skills. On the court, we're often just fourteen feet apart. (But no closer: the non-volley zone is the original social distancing mechanism.) We had better be able to get along with each other. The running commentary and frequent laughter can be as much fun as the games themselves.

Our sport is also much more accessible; age and body type are not as limiting as with some other sports. I have been able to compete and interact with players from age twelve to age eighty-two. It also recently struck me that pickleball is the only sport I have played in which I have actively competed against women, many who have as much power and more skills than me.

Speaking of accessibility, it's easier to find a game than with other sports. It can be hard to get together a golf or tennis game these days but pickleball clubs usually offer a mix of private and open-play games.

You can come down by yourself, find a game that fits your skill level, put your paddle in line, and be on the court in no time flat.

Time is another compelling advantage of pickleball. Games are "bite-sized," usually lasting around fifteen minutes or so. It's not a two-to-three-hour tennis match or a five-hour round of golf. You get to mix partners and play as few or as many games as you want. And, if you have a bad game, it's over before you know it and you get a chance for a fresh start before too long.

It's no wonder that pickleball is growing so fast. All ages and abilities can find easy access to competition and interaction. The physical and social benefits of the game promote health and connection, which are two of the factors most closely related to happiness and longevity. And the variety of the game challenges us to develop mental skills that keep us engaged (and maybe just a little addicted).

At this point, I'm tempted to get into the details of playing your best pickleball: the strokes, strategy, mental game, and secrets to bringing all of these skills together. But in deference to our friends who haven't yet figured out how to deal with us sweaty, obsessed picklers and just want to remain focused on the message of living well until they figure out that this book is just a ploy to get them to join our cult, I will ask you to wait for the Pickleball Postscript at the end of the book to delve into the essential skills and mindset that empower you to show up with your best game every day. The patience you exhibit as you wait for these pearls of wisdom will no doubt teach you the patience you need on the court to vary your shots, construct points, and wait for the right moment to finish the rally. So yes, I'm doing this for your benefit.

I hope this detour will be worth the wait.

But if you're that person who hates to wait, opens their presents on Christmas Eve, and just loves to bang the ball on every shot, feel free to skip ahead to the end (page 163) and feed your pickleball addiction. Just come back and join us so you can explore "The Art of Living" and be as serene and accepting as the rest of us when you miss your shots.

PERSPECTIVE

"We don't see things as they are, we see them as we are."
–Anais Nin

YOU ARE THE LENS THROUGH WHICH life is experienced. When your lens is in focus, you live with clarity and grace. You see clearly that you are connected, not separate. Only then can you engage with the world as a friend.

Ego and fear cloud our vision, causing us to see the outside world as a threat. When you take everything personally, every look, comment and bad bounce seems to have a sinister intent. It's crucial to realize that almost nothing others do is because of you—it's a projection of their own drama. When you lower your defenses and see the world through the prism of gratitude and oneness, your perspective shifts. You don't have to go to war with everything and everyone around you. You are merely part of life that is happening.

If you miss an easy shot, go ahead and express your frustration (with as few four-letter words as possible)—then laugh. Notice the feeling inside of you—the release of self-judgment and the freedom to accept what is and who you are. Notice the reaction of others—they will usually laugh too. We all resonate with humor, humility and perspective.

In researching this book, I had some conversations with pickleball pros to get their insights into the game. These pros acknowledged the importance of technical skills but also wanted to emphasize the mental and psychological aspects of the game. In particular, the idea of perspective was an important theme. Steve Dawson of Bobby Riggs Racket & Paddle related the story of how he competed successfully in the US Nationals shortly after having cancer surgery. For him, gratitude to be able to play at all is the perspective that defines his pickleball mindset. He also echoes one of the main themes of this book in the way he approaches tournaments: his goal is to prepare his mind and body to the fullest, then accept the results with the satisfaction that he put in the work. Winning is a distant second to doing his best.

Mark Renneson of Third Shot Sports is a fun presence in the pickleball community whether he is putting out instructional videos, coaching, or commentating on broadcasts. Part of his perspective comes from a good friend who had a brain tumor and came up with the following two rules:

1. It's not about you.
2. Sometimes it is about you, but it doesn't matter as much as you think it does.

When I spoke with Mark, I was stunned at the synchronicity of these words as I had spent the previous evening with a friend who has stage 4 pancreatic cancer. At one point my friend looked me in the eyes and said, "It's not about me." Her concern was for her kids and friends who are dealing with her condition. Brain tumors and cancer tend to outweigh the importance of such things as whether a ball clipped the line or landed just out. Rule #2 helped Mark when he had to play an important tennis match twenty minutes after finding out about a friend's death. He was able to tap into the place where competition is pure—uncontaminated by concern with results or performance anxiety. This perspective freed him to play his best.

Morgan Evans, in between relating near-death experiences, recovering from the coronavirus, and telling awesome stories that were too inappropriate to share in this book, talks about the health benefits of the game for his students. He cites leg strength and footwork developed by playing pickleball as essential factors in promoting balance, reducing falls, and promoting longevity. He also sees the mental challenge and social connection of the game as serving the same purpose—helping his older clients live healthier, vibrant lives. His perspective is informed by doing what he loves and helping others at the same time.

Irina Tereschenko is another pickleball pro who has made a successful transition from tennis, but unlike Steve, Mark, and Morgan, pickleball at this time in her life is a means to an end rather than a full-time job. Where and how often she plays has more to do with access to outdoor activities, travel destinations, or hanging out with friends she has made in the sport. She sees pickleball as less stressful than tennis, which is why you'll notice her relaxed style and easy smile as she plays. She told me that until prize money and sponsorship support create more financial incentives, she's happy to be a pickleball nomad, picking her spots and not missing out on the other passions in her life.

These accomplished players are genuinely grateful for the role this game has played in helping them make a living and providing them with an opportunity to compete, have fun, and meet great people. If the best players value gratitude and perspective above all, surely we can make this our credo as well.

PAYING IT FORWARD

Everyone with whom I spoke also mentioned the idea of "paying it forward." This aspiration is part of the charm of pickleball. It's a very supportive community. It's also a game that's past its infancy and is now in those awkward teenage years—becoming popular and growing but still learning and looking to find its place. It needs a little more time to mature, but it's starting to realize its potential.

In the meantime, most pros realize they are the ambassadors for the game; they are still approachable and relatable. If I wrote a book on tennis, as nice as they are, Federer, Nadal, and Djokovic probably wouldn't have returned my calls and been so generous with their time; nor would we be able to sign up and spend a few days with them at their camps and clinics like we can with the top pickleball players and coaches. In fact, all of us are part of a movement and play the role of pickleball ambassador when we talk with our friends and support the game. We get to appreciate the blessings that allow us to play with our friends and pay it forward. And did I mention that we get to have a helluva good time while we're securing the future of our children and making the world safe for pickleball?

AWARENESS AND COMPETENCE

Improvement on and off the court begins with awareness—clearly seeing where you are now and where you want to go. Awareness sets the stage for competence.

A useful lens through which to look at your pickleball and life journey is the "Four Stages of Competence" model. The stages are:

1. Unconscious Incompetence

In this life stage you are like a child. You don't know how to do anything and you are unaware that you don't know. This is the moment you first saw people playing pickleball and said to yourself, "Huh?"

2. Conscious Incompetence

You are painfully aware that you don't know what you're doing. This is like feeling clueless on your first date or hitting the ball over the fence and thinking that maybe a lesson or two would be a good idea.

3. Conscious Competence

You took those lessons and have played quite a bit. You know what to do but it's so damn hard to do it because you keep having to think about what you're supposed to do and end up playing mechanically and indecisively.

4. Unconscious Competence

This is where life and your game opens up as your skills become second nature. In social situations, you don't need to think your way through interactions; you just say and do the right things with confidence. This is the "flow state"—action and awareness become one, and achievement becomes effortless. On the court, you automatically end up in the right position, execute the proper shot, and seem to have the ball on a string.

Unfortunately, we all have to go through the first three stages to arrive at our destination. The goal is to spend less time in each stage along the way, reducing the suffering and increasing the joy of learning and playing. We all get stuck in certain stages. That's not an indictment of who we are; it's just that few endeavors in life are mastered. The good news is that when we make progress, our skills in one area often translate to other areas as well. This is part of the pickleball/life connection we will continue to explore together.

As you become more aware, you are in a better position to ask the right questions:
Who am I? What makes me do the things I do?
How do I bring more consistency and mindfulness to my life and game?
How do I align my body and mind to create more harmony and less anxiety?
If I try to fail, but succeed, which one did I do?

The next section of this book is devoted primarily to the process of actively assessing and creating your best self on and off the court. The connection to pickleball may not seem obvious at times but I believe that developing self-awareness and improving your life skills directly benefit your game. Optimizing your body, mind, heart, and spirit enables you to physically compete, effectively strategize, savor your experience emotionally, and see your pickleball life as being in harmony with your deepest values and self-expression.

Your relationship with concepts—such as change, challenge,

and discipline—directly affects your ability to improve and thrive. Nurturing your capacity for compassion may not help you snap the ball into your opponent's chest but it will put you in touch emotionally with their experience of being crushed by the inexorable force of pickleball nature that is you. But seriously, when you learn to recognize what's holding you back from succeeding and can explore skills that bring you understanding and lightness of heart, your experience on the court and your relationships with others will be the best they can be.

As we explore these aspects of ourselves and look to live and play our best, it's important to remember that we are creatures of habit. We have genetic blueprints and have been brought up to behave and think in certain ways. I recommend taking your standard operating system and consciously installing some updates. Reprogramming yourself with the proper awareness and techniques enables you to become the true architect of your life and game.

EMOTIONAL INTELLIGENCE

THINK OF THE QUALITIES THAT YOU admire most in someone. What comes to mind? How about this for a Top Ten?

- **Dependability**
- **Resourcefulness**
- **Kindness**
- **Patience**
- **Perseverance**
- **Fairness**
- **Creativity**
- **Discipline**
- **Humor**
- **Equanimity**

Look over the list and spend some time with these qualities or others you deem worthy. Make a conscious effort to cultivate these qualities in yourself, perhaps focusing on one area in particular each week and noticing if you sense a change in your well-being and relationships.

When I was younger, kindness, patience, and equanimity were my trouble spots. I was much more judgmental and impatient with myself and others. And my equanimity is still a work in progress as I continue to learn to accept and abide with what is. However, what has carried me along on the road to fulfillment is a dedication to the personal qualities I value most.

What is the one skill I would recommend cultivating to live productively and happily? What is the source that unlocks the wonderful qualities listed above? It's emotional intelligence, or EI, as I like to call it. Like artificial intelligence (AI), it is powerful and world changing. Developing emotional intelligence is much of what this book is about. A world imbued with EI is a world that is more peaceful, compassionate, cooperative, and joyful. All of the subjects in this book flow from the wellspring of emotional intelligence.

We all know people who are really smart and we know people who work very hard. However, show me someone who is able to manage relationships, say the right thing at the right time, make people feel comfortable, engender trust, and act with a combination of humility and confidence, and chances are the world is their oyster. This is EI in a nutshell—the ability to use, understand, and manage your own emotions in a positive way.

It's essential to develop emotional intelligence if you want to live in flow and harmony with others. Identifying virtuous qualities gives us guideposts to travel our path to contentment and fulfillment. While it's often easy to appreciate these characteristics in others, we often don't cultivate them in ourselves—then wonder why we seem discontent and irritated with life.

EI in business means valuing everyone you encounter, not just the customer, but suppliers, employees, and competitors alike. It means identifying a need and respectfully and conscientiously responding to it. In relationships, it means living the Golden Rule—caring deeply about others and giving more than you get. In your inner life, emotional intelligence is living by the Serenity Prayer—cultivating the wisdom to change what you can and accepting what you cannot. It means doing the work to see yourself with clarity and mindfully bringing your higher self into the world for the benefit of all. On the court, as in life, it's treating your partners and competitors with dignity and appreciation; we tap our paddles at game's end as an expression of respect and gratitude for the time spent together.

THE SECRET SAUCE

But how do you develop and embody the qualities that emanate from emotional intelligence? First you need to take these qualities and make them your own—consciously develop an emotionally intelligent mindset. It will require a lot of attention, but through focused practice it will become a habit that brings these qualities to the forefront of your mind and defines your character for all to see.

Here is the proper mindset to take your unique set of personal qualities and use them to create your best possible life. Ready? Here it comes. Drum roll . . .

Try hard. Have fun. Play nice.

When we do these three things we know that we are putting in the effort, not taking ourselves too seriously, and treating others well. This advice may sound like something you would tell children, but simplicity has a way of cutting through to the truth. When people ask me about my kids, I give them the usual relationship and job status info. But I also point out that what I'm most proud of is that they try to do their best and are kindhearted.

You may realize already that there are parts of yourself that could improve. Who knew?! Specifically, maybe you are not eating and exercising as you would like. Maybe you aren't challenging yourself intellectually and have become more comfortable being constantly entertained than exploring opportunities to learn. Perhaps the quality of your relationships could use some more attention. Is there anyone you are taking for granted? Have you put off reaching out to someone you care about because you're too busy? And finally, are there spiritual aspects that long to be nourished and would bring greater meaning to what can sometimes seem like an endless routine of doing and striving without much purpose? These are the "try hard" parts of your life where targeted effort is required to thrive physically, intellectually, emotionally, and spiritually. The rewards are obvious: you operate at a higher level and your sense of balance enables you to see and seize opportunities when they arise.

Having fun depends on how you see the personal work that lies before you. Is it a chore to devote attention to these aspects of your life or is it a joy to connect and excel? Fine-tuning and improving your life and your game requires energy and discipline. It's sometimes easier to just sit back and veg out, but devoting energy to worthwhile pursuits can generate more energy than is expended on the front end. The key is to actively notice and enjoy how your life improves when you put in the effort. Hard work is required but it can actually be a fun undertaking. The joy of living your best life is the gift that keeps on giving.

Playing nice means that when your head hits the pillow at night, you don't have to lie awake in a state of guilt or regret. You will know that you have played fair, spoken your truth, and gone out of your way to show kindness and affection to others. No matter what financial success or social status you achieve, playing nice is the ultimate scoreboard in my book. Long after you finish the game, people will forget if you won or lost; they won't remember how you spent your money; they will remember how you treated them. When I think of the people I respect most, kindness and a sense of decency are nonnegotiable requirements. Achievement is admirable. Treating others well along the way raises success to the level of fulfillment.

FINDING YOU ARE ENOUGH

Finding you are enough does not mean you don't strive for excellence. It's not about settling. Personally, I love to feel that I am excelling and pushing boundaries. We admire great athletes, entertainers, and entrepreneurs. They are often specialists who can block out certain aspects of their lives and use tunnel vision to master their chosen pursuits. If you want to be a concert violinist or brain surgeon, your idea of balance needs to be different than what I recommend for us regular folks trying to improve our dinks and have a good time—your "enough" had better be extraordinary.

That's my point: pickleball can be challenging, but it ain't brain surgery. It's not life or death—and neither are many things in your life that you stress about. *Problems arise when the joy of the journey is undermined by an unhealthy fixation on perfection, results, or external validation.*

You can become a very good player but feel miserable because you don't play your best every game. You can play a great game but that young guy with his damn young reflexes gets the better of you. If someone is outperforming you in some way in spite of your best efforts, there is peace to be found not in giving up or being resentful, but in sincerely and humbly acknowledging and celebrating great talent. Chances are that if you have put in the work and the time, you will have done pretty well.

Sometimes you expend great effort but the results are slow to come. It takes patience and trust that things will work out, even if it seems like the rewards will never manifest. If some aspect of your life is not what you want it to be, take a moment to let yourself off the hook. Life is hard. Keep trying but be grateful for what you have instead of being bitter for what you don't. It may sound trite, but a little love and self-compassion go a long way. Put in the effort, be kind to yourself and others, and let the chips fall where they may. Enjoy the miracle and good fortune of being alive and getting to play a game.

"Enough" may sound like a static concept, but it is actually dynamic. Embrace the paradox of being content but continuing to explore and seek.

The quest to be better is not a condemnation of who you are—it is an opportunity to find new versions of yourself that may be *even more* satisfying and fulfilling.

FINDING *YOUR* ENOUGH

This is slightly different than finding ***you're*** enough. As you try to incorporate some of the steps discussed in this book, remember that change is difficult—*really* difficult. We all have different talents and histories. Some of us struggle with our physical abilities while others could care less about spiritual pursuits. It's all good. Only you know what ***your*** enough looks and feels like.

The worst outcome is that you end up frustrated and less happy than when you started because you don't feel like you are measuring up to the challenge of change. Celebrate progress—you're still a winner if you're doing your best and enjoying the game of pickleball and the game of life. Appreciate what you *can* do instead of obsessing about what comes more slowly or not at all. This is not a test that you pass or fail. Don't let unrealistic expectations derail the real progress and happiness available to you. As long as you put in the effort and enjoy the experience, then it's all good. Your enough is enough, no matter what.

TOUCHSTONES

Remember when I said I wouldn't come up with a catchy ten-step program like a lot of self-help books? Okay, I lied. But there are only seven steps here, so I just stretched the truth. Or as a politician or celebrity would say after getting caught in a lie or a screwup—"I misspoke," "Someone hacked my Twitter account," and "That's not who I am." (No, you didn't. Probably not. Yeah, it kinda is.)

The following steps were introduced at the outset of this book.

Now that you have more context and information, let's dive a little deeper . . .

Assess Yourself

What you do is inextricable from who you are—if you want to do great things, you must build a great self. Honest self-assessment precedes meaningful progress. Some aspects of seeing yourself can be painful; most of us are harder on ourselves than we are on anyone else. But it can also be fun and instructive to look at your flaws and laugh at yourself—just a little. Let your guard down a bit. The people who matter the most will still love us in spite of our shortcomings. Extend that same courtesy to yourself.

Honestly assessing and reflecting on where you are now will show you where you want to go. This is not the time for shortcuts. Devote the time needed to build self-awareness before embarking on game- and life-improving strategies. Otherwise you might find yourself doing the Springsteen Shuffle (one step up and two steps back).

Understand the Interplay of Mind and Emotion

The unobserved mind is incapable of directing conscious change. Unobserved emotions can sabotage any rational plan. Meditation and self-assessment bring this interplay into focus. You come to understand the emotional origin of thoughts—and you see that thoughts are passing clouds in the sky of your consciousness. Any practice that enables you to step back and see these truths more clearly is the gateway to wisdom.

Develop a Growth Mindset

As you embrace challenge, exert effort without obsessing about results, persist in the face of setbacks, learn from criticism, and believe you have the power to change who you are for the better, you set yourself on a course to reach your greatest potential. Belief in your power to shape your experience of life is the precursor to personal growth and achievement. Belief in the power to improve your pickleball skills keeps pickleball instructors in business. Thank you, Growth Mindset!

Engage Your Higher Self

When you pause and *act* from a place of wisdom rather than reflexively *react* to every fleeting thought or emotion, your life unfolds in alignment with your values and purpose. Pausing to see clearly gives your higher self the opportunity to be your guide rather than operating from a place of ego, desire, and fear. You rise up and become the architect of your life.

Create "Success Environments"

Consciously building virtuous habits provides a framework to achieve success. Bad habits need to be replaced with new patterns that create healthy environments and yield positive results. When you fall back into old habits that you want to change, don't be too hard on yourself. Keep the self-scolding to a minimum. Just notice it and gently remind yourself that this is a journey of discovery. Willpower comes and goes—discipline and habits help you stay the course and live your best with less drama and effort.

Develop Perspective and Self-Compassion

Striving without perspective can leave you dissatisfied no matter what you achieve in life. Self-compassion is the antidote to self-judgment. Engage your sense of perspective when you feel yourself obsessing about temporary phenomena, news cycles, or your pickleball game. Things will change. In the meantime, don't give away your life wrapped up in what is beyond your control or living in the misery of guilt and self-judgment.

Live in the Present Moment

Intense noticing is at the heart of the concept of presence. When you are caught up in thought, it is almost impossible to turn your focus to the world around you. Clearing your mind through meditation or intention creates space to engage fully with whomever or whatever you choose.

Remember that unconscious competence is the state we aspire to on the court—a flow state in which you are effortlessly engaged in the present moment and playing your best. You aren't thinking about making shots. Even better, you're not thinking about pandemics, politics, or your neighbor's kid with the new drum set. No wonder we love pickleball and other sports!

Another treasure that the present moment offers is appreciation for the wonder of life unfolding right now: the miracle of consciousness, the glory of nature, a pickleball zooming between your surprised opponents. There are so many stories rattling around in your head right now that do not serve you—they only agitate and distract. Return to the present moment and reclaim your experience of what it feels like to be alive instead of thinking about what it feels like to be alive.

These seven principles will help you realize your potential, live your values, and find peace of mind. These principles are the touchstones of your foundation. Check in with yourself often. When you feel overwhelmed or lost, come back to these basics and recommit to the process of living mindfully and taking care of yourself.

> If you would like to explore these seven touchstones in more detail, I offer short talks on each of these subjects at mikebranon.com. I would welcome your feedback on how you see the role these touchstones play in your life.

BUILDING A FOUNDATION

As a former contractor, I am painfully aware of what happens if you don't build on a solid foundation. Everything above the surface becomes more complicated and out of alignment. However, it's possible to take a systematic approach to building your foundation. Body, mind, heart and spirit are familiar building blocks, and with some motivation, discipline and imagination, you can build an amazing life with them. If you are ready to take on the challenge to live and play better, let's back up the cement mixer and start pouring that foundation right now.

"TRY HARD": THE PHYSICAL FOUNDATION

"You can't expect to look like a million bucks if you eat from the dollar menu."

– *Anonymous*

If you want to give your best on the court, you have to be your best off the court. You can try as hard as you can but if your body isn't cooperating, it's going to be a tougher task. There have been countless books written on diet and exercise. Infomercials, multilevel marketing campaigns, weight-loss programs, and gyms comprise an industry worth billions of dollars. Yet obesity is rising steadily as is its cohort, diabetes. *In 2020, 83 percent of men and 72 percent of women will be overweight or obese. Over 10 percent of Americans have diabetes.*[1] I'm not a medical professional but even I can tell that something is terribly wrong. Too often, we think that the more complex or challenging the solution, the more legitimate it is. But really, the "prescription" is simple:

Eat well. Keep moving.

EAT WELL

I know you are aware of this already, yet many people continue to jeopardize their health because of bad information or lack of a coherent plan. If you managed a business like many people manage their health, you would go bankrupt. Without structure, you are doomed to fail; wanting to do well only goes so far. There are always rationalizations that undermine good health. In studies where people self-report about their diet they almost always under-report what and how much they eat. Only a food diary will give you accurate feedback. Have your partner, or better yet, a nutritionist look over your entries. If they start laughing, chances are you forgot to write down the carne asada burrito, chips, and soda you labeled as an afternoon "snack."

There is no need for hunger; just eat better food. When you feel deprived, you will seek ways to avoid that feeling. A coherent plan must be specific, achievable, and measurable. Have that friend or partner

[1]Obesity Projections Worse than Terrorism Threat for Future--and We Can Do Something about It." Women's Health Research Institute, February 11, 2015. https://womenshealth.obgyn.msu.edu/blog/obesity-projections-worse-terrorism-threat-future-and-we-can-do-something-about-it.

review that plan with you. A good plan should serve as motivation rather than feel like deprivation. Revamping your nutrition plan doesn't happen overnight. Eating is a great social experience and if there are some foods you enjoy with friends and family that may have accidentally fallen into a frying pan, that's okay. Remember what I said in the beginning: nobody is perfect. You might have to push the reset button on your plan several times. The important thing is, wait for it . . . progress. Not perfection. Sound familiar? I have cut way back on red meat and added more vegetables to my diet. But pulled pork sandwiches and the occasional rogue chalupa still find their way onto my plate. I wish I was a dedicated vegetarian but it's something I'm still working on. If you are in a high-risk group for diabetes or heart disease, I really hope you can make a big change because we like having you around.

It's hard to change the way you eat but the rewards are numerous. You will feel better about yourself. Your mind will be sharper. And your healthier body will enable you to play your best game. Healthy eating can be a high wire act—temptation can easily knock you off balance. Develop a plan. Eat well. Feel better.

KEEP MOVIING

"A body at rest tends to remain at rest. A body in motion tends to stay in motion."

– Sir Isaac Newton

"I like to move it, move it!"

– King Julien in the movie Madagascar (Original artist: Reel 2 Real)

The author, with his role model, King Julien. Author on left.

(Editor's note: Most authors pose in front of a bookcase in their study, wearing a sensible sweater and a contemplative gaze. This one looks like a big four-year-old at an amusement park. We take no responsibility for the contents of this book other than dealing with the author's questionable grammar skills.)

It's no coincidence that modern life has turned us into sitting dorks. Video stimuli and work environments encourage a sedentary lifestyle. Movement is the most basic way to fight back against this trend—moving around a court with a paddle in your hand chasing a little plastic ball is even better. When you move, your muscles literally squeeze blood and lymph throughout your body, improving your circulation and immune systems. If you are unable to avoid sitting for long periods of time, simply set a timer on your phone that prompts you to get up and move around for a couple of minutes every half hour. Take deep breaths and stretch often.

When you move less, your body adapts to that state. You are telling your body that it is winter and it's time to slow down metabolism and store fat. Circulation is reduced. Brain function is diminished. Muscles atrophy. Dr. James Levine of the Mayo Clinic coined the phrase, "Sitting is the new smoking." Prolonged sitting or lying down increases the risk of heart disease, stroke, diabetes, and some cancers.

Now that you are jogging in place while you read out of sheer terror, let's talk about the role of movement in your pickleball game. Proper movement is the difference between getting all the way to the kitchen line after your return of serve and getting caught while still moving in no man's land. It's the difference between getting in position to execute every fundamental shot and reaching awkwardly for balls just outside of your reach. If you watch the best pickleball and tennis pros, they are almost always in the optimal position to execute each shot. Half the battle is getting there and you can't get there if your fitness level and positioning are inadequate.

Another vital aspect is your flexibility. Not only does flexibility allow you to get to more shots and bend your knees, it protects you from injury. *The only thing worse than not playing well is not playing at all.* If you want to be in the proper posture at the net, add some squats and lunges to your exercise routine to maintain that low, balanced position.

You must set aside specific time in your schedule for movement and exercise; what doesn't get scheduled usually doesn't happen. As you know by now, willpower isn't enough. If you're a devoted pickler, you're probably doing pretty well. If you're not, put together a structured program or come join us on the courts.

This is not an exercise book even though it is one of my passions. There is plenty of information out there. Do some research on proper exercise or ask a trusted friend who looks halfway decent. (Just tell your friend how good they look and they will fall all over themselves to try and help you.)

STRETCH

Have you ever stopped to notice that stretching just *feels good*? Animals reflexively stretch when they awaken or get ready to move. You might actually purr when you stretch because it feels so unexpectedly pleasant after sitting for long periods. (Or maybe that's just me ... why is everybody staring at me?)

I experienced a pain crisis stage in my thirties when years of long office hours, competitive basketball, and weightlifting without proper stretching left me unable to even get out of bed or into a car at times. I remember once while on vacation in Mexico, I ended up flat on my back on a sidewalk, unable to get up. (And no, it wasn't the tequila that time.) Out of desperation and hoping to avoid surgery, I went to massage therapy school and became a licensed therapist. I wanted to be able to help others, but to be honest, I was primarily trying to figure out how to regain my own health. The good news is that it worked. I haven't had major back problems for almost twenty years now and live a full and active life. It's a true blessing that fills me with gratitude.

Remember to move with breath. Deep breaths help expand the stretch. Extend the stretch within your comfort zone on the exhale. Feel the sensation of lengthening your body while bathing your circulatory and lymphatic systems in nourishing oxygen. Continue to stretch for small moments during the day, even while sitting. The cue system is something that works for me. I am reminded to stretch and take a deep breath when I come to a stoplight, hit send on an email, or have an impure thought about [YOUR LEAST FAVORITE POLITICIAN HERE]. (That last one has really helped my flexibility lately.)

Do what works for you. I have refined my stretching system and taught it to others. Unfortunately, it's too hard to explain here without showing you a video of me in my sassy Lululemon stretching outfit. (Just use your imagination. It's breathtaking.) If you would rather not use your imagination, check out my stretching program and other fitness tips at mikebranon.com.

CARDIO

Walk briskly at least thirty minutes a day, five days a week—a heart rate between 50 to 80 percent of maximum is optimal. Run if your joints and conditioning allow, but walking is just fine. Simple movement of any kind improves circulation and mood. Start at your own level and work your way up to where you want to be. (Stop me if you've heard this but there's this odd game called pickleball that gets your heart pumping too.)

Walking with a friend, coworker, or family member can make exercise fun and invite closeness. My wife and I have some of our best conversations while walking together. The usual distractions of home, office, and electronic devices are gone. Space is created to talk and enjoy being outside together. Again, the more fun you're having, the more likely you will keep doing it.

BREATHE

Intentional breathing is one of the best things you can do for yourself, and it's hiding in plain sight. It's not expensive and takes up no extra time because chances are you're breathing anyway. Deep breathing reduces stress, stimulates the immune system, and improves your mood. Not breathing can result in less desirable outcomes such as immediate death. But seriously, pausing to take several deep breaths can be rejuvenating and relaxing. Go ahead and try a few right now and feel the sensation.

When you are stressed or feel lethargic try standing up and taking a few deep breaths and move. Feed your body with oxygen. It's gluten free and available now. Operators (and your lungs) are standing by.

RESISTANCE TRAINING

As we age, we lose muscle mass. Fight back with resistance training. Lean muscle literally burns energy and fat even at rest. The time you spend building muscle is multiplied by the time muscle works for you. Again, do your research. Consider getting a program from a personal trainer or online. Don't adhere to the "no pain, no gain" philosophy, especially if you are not a top athlete. Injury and pain will sidetrack you in a heartbeat. It's all about consistency and proper technique.

If you have not been resistance training, start slowly. A little soreness is fine. You are waking up muscles that have been snoozing for a while. We're not looking at Schwarzeneggerian results. (I'm pretty sure that's a real word.) We are after tone and functional strength; this is what allows us to look good and navigate our world with physical confidence.

Recent graduate of my resistance-training class. Before & After.

YOGA

My wife, Diane, has never considered herself to be an athlete but she loves her yoga. It gives her a way to feed her physical self without having to go out and compete with others. (No, she doesn't play pickleball. She would rather lose than hit a ball at somebody and have them be offended.) Yoga fills a social purpose as well when she practices with a friend or a group. It's also easier on her joints than the kind of sports that I enjoy. But I think her favorite part of yoga is when her dorky husband joins her and she gets to watch him occasionally fall over or cramp up trying to do what she does effortlessly. Regardless, a yoga practice covers a lot of bases and can be a worthwhile part of your fitness routine. A good online source for yoga instruction is *Yoga with Adriene* on YouTube. It's free and she is all about making yoga accessible to everyone.

I OBJECT, YOUR HONOR!

We love to see righteous lawyers in courtroom dramas stand up and passionately defend their clients. Maybe your inner lawyer is making a case against my suggestions as you read; you know it's important, but you don't have the time and energy to do all this stuff. I get it—I won't overrule your objection. Life can be demanding and time can be in short supply. But consider this:

- You don't have to do everything at once. Just do *something* now. Pick a category or two to start and see where it goes from there. You can find free yoga and strength-training programs online and walking, stretching, and breathing aren't taxable activities (yet).

- Time is short but I have developed abbreviated programs that keep me on track when necessary. You can improve your health in each category in less time than you might think.

  Stretching/yoga: 10 minutes. I have devised a stretching routine that incorporates elements of yoga. My "Geez, I gotta be out the door in ten minutes" routine keeps me flexible and rejuvenated. I also do stretches while I am at the computer or watching TV: extra time required = 0 minutes. Be creative—you can do the same thing.

  Cardio: 30 minutes. There's no magic shortcut for this, but something is better than nothing and more is better. Increase your walking pace during normal activities. Schedule walking conversations or meetings with family members or coworkers. Get out of your chair for brief periods when working or online.

  Core workout: 6 minutes. The Athlean-X YouTube channel offers videos that will challenge you at your level and give you results in no time flat (abs).

  Resistance training: 15 minutes. You can do a full-body workout with circuit training in this time frame. Google "circuit training" and modify the programs to fit your time requirements.

The same formula can apply to fitting meditation into your schedule. (Check out *8 Minute Meditation* by Victor Davich.) None of these shortcuts require commuting or gym memberships. Just make sure you schedule it. Add it to your phone's calendar, write it down in a planner, set an alarm—just schedule it, like you would any other activity. What you don't schedule gets put aside. I guarantee you will feel and play better.

BODY/MIND CONNECTION

This just in! The body and the mind are connected. You know this of course, because your hands are holding this book/reader while your mind is being blown every minute as you read on. Consistent aerobic exercise induces neuroplasticity (more on that soon) and facilitates improved cognitive functions. So the next time you go out for a walk, just remember that you're getting smarter with every step you take. If you walk far enough you will begin to understand the Theory of Relativity and why the Kardashians are so popular.

Anyway, the science is in. This stuff works. Assessing your physical self is critically important. It really *can* be a matter of life and death. It surely is a difference maker when it comes to playing your best, feeling healthy and strong, and improving your emotional and intellectual well-being. Besides the physical problems caused by a poor diet and lack of fitness, psychological problems can creep in as well. Even if you are successful in other aspects of your life, you can be left feeling dissatisfied with who you are. You now have more solid information. All that's left to do is to make a plan similar to the one I have laid out above that fits *your* circumstances and approach it with the right mindset. If you want to achieve a "flow state" in your life, good health is the first step in building a solid personal foundation.

OPTIONAL ACTION PLAN

A Harvard Business Study found that the 3 percent of graduates from their MBA program who had their goals written down ended up earning ten times as much as the other 97 percent put together, just ten years after graduation.[2]

There are many other studies that document the efficacy of writing down your goals and tracking them over time, and if you are motivated to do so you can develop an action plan. Start a journal. It can be an actual journal or an online document. Divide it into sections that deal with eating and exercise plans.

Let's get you started.

What are your strengths?

____

____

____

What would you like to improve?

____

____

____

Your exercise program should consist of specific days and times when you will stretch, move, and resistance train.

---

[2] Acton, Annabel. Harvard Business Study. "How to Set Goals (and Why You Should Write Them Down). November 3, 2017.

Workout day:

Notes:

Stretch day:

Notes:

Resistance Training:

Notes:

Other Activity:

Notes:

Start slowly and work your way up to levels that continue to challenge you as you progress. Leave plenty of space after each entry to fill in more details later.

You can also incorporate or keep a separate pickleball journal with tips you've picked up from lessons or online content. I can tell you from experience that this is a great way to consolidate what you already know and bring that awareness to the court. It's also beneficial to write about especially good days when you may have stumbled upon something that really made your game shine. In addition, you can include funny stories about your playing partners or memorable points to look back on later and relive the good times that might have otherwise faded away.

Make it fun. It's essential that you enjoy the process rather than use these entries to criticize yourself. Improvement doesn't happen overnight. It's going to require a mix of patience and tough love to get where you need to go. Providing structure and building new habits will keep you on track on those days when your body tries to grab the keys and make a run for the ice cream shop down the street when your willpower isn't looking.

When your body is ready to operate at a higher level—well fed, well rested, and with improved strength and flexibility—your game has a solid foundation on which to build your skills. You will live a healthier life. What could possibly sabotage your plans? It might be that space between your ears where good intentions lose their way.

Laying out your fitness and nutrition goals is one thing, but how do you get your mind to actually execute those goals? Rewiring your brain to lead the charge and take you where you want to go is the second half of the "Try Hard" plan.

TRY HARD II: (not starring Bruce Willis) THE MENTAL FUNDAMENTALS

"Live as if you were to die tomorrow. Learn as if you were to live forever."

– Mahatma Gandhi

CONSIDER THE DIFFERENCE BETWEEN "mindless" and "mindful." Where you fall on the spectrum between these two opposites dramatically influences where you end up in life. Again, most of us know what to do but have trouble actually executing—it's that gap between **knowing** and **doing** that determines our outcomes. When you hear someone say, "I know I should exercise more," that simply means their mind hasn't been able to develop the habits or willpower needed to achieve positive outcomes. When you hear someone say that they should have dinked that ball around their ankles instead of hit it hard into the net, it means that their mind has not been sufficiently trained to hit low balls soft and high balls hard. There's really not a lot of time to think on the court at times; the better players just have ingrained habits that result in superior shot selection and optimal decisions time after time. Successful people do the same thing in all aspects of their lives.

Engage your mind to build good habits and find ways to challenge yourself. Explore music, foreign languages, or other topics that sound interesting. Great Courses Plus is an excellent source for online courses that cover a wide spectrum of topics. It's like going to a college class, but you can hang out in your PJs and make snarky comments about the professor. And the University of YouTube is chock-full of instruction on almost any subject you want to take on from home repair to medieval history to third-shot drops.

You can join groups to explore spirituality, discuss good books and shared interests, or just have some good conversations. Learning keeps you vibrant and interesting. I am often surprised to find that I have internalized things I have learned but no longer remember reading about until I come across them again. Neuroplasticity is the process by which your brain physically changes in response to what you occupy it with. If you feed it with good things, it adapts and grows in that direction. You literally become what you think and do. It's a great example of the possibility of changing your reality with virtuous habits at any age.

Consider rediscovering the joy of learning. You may feel some latent resistance because it reminds you of school assignments or work requirements—learning on some level can feel like a chore. The word "homework" still carries a negative connotation for many of us. But when you watch someone learn and acquire new pickleball or life skills, they light up.

What you learn will reshape your life.

LIFE SKILLS

When I taught high school psychology, I always tried to sneak life skills into the mix. I remember teaching behaviorism or Jungian theory and occasionally seeing the distracted looks on my students' faces. But when I related psychology to finances, self-analysis, or dealing with friends and family, the energy and attention in the room was always high.

Life skills should be an essential part of every high school curriculum. Self-awareness, conflict management, nutrition, and financial literacy are just a few of the topics that would better prepare our young people to navigate life's challenges. I hope someday to find like-minded educators or parents and offer a course or at least a series of seminars that would explore these concepts. It could give our kids a head start in dealing with real issues that can improve their lives. I just wish I knew then what I know now but I didn't know that I didn't know what to know then. Right?

Acquiring skills may take work but it is such a pleasure. Whether it's perfecting a new shot that befuddles your opponents or figuring out how to use a new app on your phone, learning gives us a purpose that enriches our days. We evolved to meet challenges; if challenges don't overwhelm us, they make us feel alive.

YOUR RELATIONSHIP WITH "CHALLENGE"

> "The ultimate measure of a man is not where he stands in moments of comfort and convenience, but where he stands at times of challenge and controversy."
>
> – *Dr. Martin Luther King, Jr.*

Do you expect life not to be challenging? Are you taken aback when it is? Imagine life without any challenges. How boring. If you played in games in which you effortlessly won every time, it would become unsatisfying in no time flat. With players around your own level, you are compelled to train hard, focus intently, and develop skills to compete successfully. If all that mattered was winning and not having to excel, you could find a game playing against some young kids and just dominate, although you might get some strange looks from their parents.

On some level I think most of us enjoy challenges. It gives you the opportunity to employ what you have learned to find solutions. Nothing is more satisfying than keeping your cool, dissecting a difficult situation, and making the most out of it. When challenges arise, you spend less time in denial and panic mode and proceed directly to constructive action and mindful attention to the problem at hand. When your pickleball game reaches this level, you are calmly anticipating where the ball is headed as you read the angle of your opponent's paddle. Your footwork consistently puts you in the right position. You execute the proper shot at the right time.

Best of all, you don't have to even think about it! It just happens because you have taken on the challenge of building your physical and mental skillset.

Admittedly some challenges are actually very stressful. Trying to make rent after getting laid off is not as fun as figuring out how to improve your backhand. But each situation requires ingenuity and hard work.

I have slept on floors and in my car. I have lived on Top Ramen and worked minimum wage jobs to get by. I have been rejected for jobs that I was overqualified for and made poor financial decisions. But hardships and failure are the learning experiences that we remember the most. I wouldn't trade those experiences for anything because those rough spots showed me I could meet a challenge, survive, and come back stronger next time.

Chances are that you have had some similar experiences. Many people are eager to talk about their successes but it can be illuminating to share your fears and failures with a trusted friend. We learn that we aren't the only ones who have struggled. If we don't give up, our experience empowers us to meet every new challenge with an attitude that wastes little time on melodrama and instead focuses energy on solutions and strategies. Gratitude and perspective become our allies when we look back at hard times and see how we met the challenge and came out the other side. These "failures" give us confidence that we will give our best no matter what awaits us.

Some problems can't be solved, only managed. We never choose to seek out problems but when they find us, we can learn to recognize them and meet them head on with equanimity. This is the value of our experience. We won't always win, but we can cope and persevere with dignity. Problems don't define us; it's our reaction to them that reveals our true character.

When you are first met with your next challenge, try to be present—take time to see if your reaction to challenge is negative. When the problem arises, how much time do you spend complaining or feeling victimized? It's natural to have a reflex reaction to an unforeseen setback. You're only human. But how long does it take from the initial feeling to moving forward and meeting the challenge with whatever resources you have available? This is your opportunity to practice the skills you have developed over a lifetime. This is the time to take constructive action and build even more self-confidence for the next challenge that will surely come your way.

Life, like pickleball, is a challenge. It has always been that way throughout the evolution of our species. The art of living and playing well is to meet the inevitable challenges with the right state of mind. Acknowledge the difficulty. Seek help when needed. Speak your truth as kindly and clearly as possible. Embrace the "not knowing" and give it your best without expectation of reward. Strive for excellence without being consumed or demeaned by it. If a problem was partly your fault, own up to it and find ways to change that require less need for forgiveness in the future.

CHANGE

Many people think of change as a four-letter word. Those people are not good at counting letters. But our attitudes about change affect our lives in a big way. Some of us are very resistant to the very idea of change. I tried to convince my mom to get and use a cell phone. No matter what advantages I explained, she was resistant to the idea. Same thing with recording shows so she didn't have to sit through commercials and could watch what she wanted at her leisure and not miss her favorite shows and blah, blah, blah . . . It just wasn't going to happen. And I'm sure my kids with all their new-fangled Snapgram, Tweeter and Instachat thingies will have similar conversations with me not too long from now.

Sameness can be comforting. We have built patterns in our life that help us spend our days efficiently and dependably; there's nothing new to figure out. Tradition is another way of warding off change. ("Why do you do that?" "It's what I've always done.") Sameness simplifies life. Until change becomes the new normal, it complicates life; so resistance to change is understandable. As they say, "Better the devil you know than the devil you don't." And there are real benefits to having more predictability in an unpredictable world. But sometimes, sameness just means "stuck."

When you analyze the aspects of yourself and see which parts need more care and feeding, you empower yourself to make changes that bring greater fulfillment. And you reduce the suffering you experience brought on by resistance to sensible change. Sometimes you can be completely unaware of what the benefits of change can feel like. You can get used to and even cling to behaviors that are self-damaging because of fear of the unknown. The key is to find an equilibrium between enjoying the life that you have put together and becoming trapped by parts of it that no longer serve you. Once again it takes attention, awareness, and a bit of courage to find your optimal balance. Impermanence is the true nature of life. Everything changes and our resistance to that fact causes suffering. When we are open to change we become open to the possibility of reinventing ourselves and our world for the better.

DISCIPLINE

Think of how you would end up if you:

- Ate and drank whatever you wanted whenever you wanted.
- Did whatever you wanted without regard for anyone else.
- Bought whatever you wanted whenever you felt the urge.
- Played video games or watched TV all day.
- Hit shots without a strategic plan.

You might get some temporary satisfaction but you would end up obese, alone, broke, unhealthy, and on the losing end of a lot of pickleball games. You would probably feel lethargic and empty at the end of the day. Discipline is a funny thing. We tend to resist the idea of it and equate it with punishment. Yet think of how you feel at the end of the day when you have lived in a disciplined way. You feel a sense of well-being and accomplishment. Embracing discipline helps you feel that you are living your values. You attract others into your orbit who are high functioning and supportive.

Self-discipline is a great virtue. Picture someone in your mind who possesses this quality. It's hard not to admire that trait. This person probably exudes an inner strength and a sense of purpose. They are confident. They are rarely waylaid by temptations and probably are successful at whatever they set their mind to accomplish.

When we develop self-discipline we can overcome negative habits that may have seeped into our lives. We can assess, make a plan, and carry it out without getting derailed by distractions. A good plan is discipline's little helper. If you find that your discipline tends to waver, it's even more important to make rules and incorporate them into a plan that keeps you on course.

Discipline also tells you when you have had enough. It is not mindless striving without end. Rather, it is a focus on identifying and reaching the place where you are enough. Wise effort seeks to find a balance between settling and obsession.

The goal is not mastery to the point of misery.

Many players work hard, drill, and do everything in their power to unlock their potential on the court. I admire that kind of discipline, but if they think hard work translates to mastery or perfection, they are bound to be disappointed and unhappy on some level. You can do all the right things, but sometimes, *you just miss.* That's pickleball. That's life.

It's vital to realize that discipline doesn't have to be practiced with a set jaw and a scowl on your face. Repeat after me: discipline is not a punishment. At its best, it flows freely from a place of optimistic determination to live and play well. It can be joyous as well as fulfilling. When you're thriving because of your focus on worthy goals, life feels good. This energy lifts you up and carries others along with you.

When you get older, you will fall somewhere on the spectrum between living a good life full of connection, health, and accomplishments, or regret that you squandered your opportunities. There may be a lot of time to look back on your life. Don't waste it. Now is the only time you have to reinforce good habits or replace bad ones. Find your sense of joyful discipline and watch life open up before you. Disciplined people are happier in the long run than those who can't visualize their future selves and become victims of instant gratification.

SHORT-TERM THINKING

Instant gratification is a powerful urge. That little "pleasure demon" on your right shoulder can lock the "wisdom angel" on your left shoulder in the closet and start whispering in your ear:

- *"Ya know what goes great with Reality TV? A pint of Ben & Jerry's. Don't forget to lick the lid!"*
- *"Yes you have a lot of shoes. But those sparkly blue ones? OMG! Credit cards are da bomb."*
- *"Exercise hard. Couch good."*

We are assaulted more than ever by offers for immediate gratification, whether it's from advertisers, click-hungry websites, or fast-food companies. It's difficult to maintain a long-term perspective when it seems like everyone around you is getting what they want now. The impact of this phenomenon is like the proverbial frog in slowly heated water that doesn't realize there's a problem until it's too late. One day, you wake up overweight, out of shape, overstressed, in debt, and with health problems or addictions that can become life-altering or life-ending. The time to act is *now* even if it means passing on some immediate gratification. It can be hard work and feel daunting to change bad habits but long-term thinking is the only way to win the race. It's a lot harder to lose fifty pounds than five pounds, and it's much easier to get more movement and flexibility if you already have some to start with.

Temporary pleasure rather than lasting happiness is what many people are chasing in this world, but immediate gratification is a fool's game. The more you get now, the less it feels good and the quicker the feeling of satisfaction fades. Pleasure leaves you looking for your next hit. And there are plenty of companies lining up to be your pleasure pusher. Your intellectual self knows this to be true. Your emotions and desires need a chaperone or they will eat, drink, spend, and chase pleasure like a sailor on shore leave.

So if you want immediate gratification, start getting your kicks in the present by taking a few moments to enjoy how you feel when you eat well, exercise, or connect with someone in your life on a deep level.

Feel the difference between mindlessly feeding a desire and living well.

Take time to notice how it feels when you have made healthy choices during your day. Use pickleball as an example to give yourself credit for the good habits you develop while continuing to work on strategies to improve the times when you are still in the process of trying to reach your goals.

Your mind is a wonder. Take care of yours by understanding how it works, how to make it function better, and seeing what unexamined notions can get in the way of sound thinking. You can approach your world and your game with intellectual curiosity and feed your innate thirst to learn. By doing so you expand your horizons, improve your game, and become more vibrant and interesting in the process. You also can learn to orient your intellect toward the virtues of discipline, to take on challenge with the proper mindset, to recognize the pitfalls of immediate gratification, and to embrace change as a path to creating the life you choose.

Mindfulness, long-term thinking, and perseverance are what will set you apart in a short-attention–span world.

PERSEVERANCE: WORKING ON YOUR MASTERPIECE WHEN EVERYTHING AROUND YOU IS GOING TO HELL

A common bond among books that seek ways to improve the quality of life is advocating the development of skills; you build your life with skills. When you see a musician sit down at a piano and play a beautiful sonata or watch a pickleball pro hit a series of perfect shots, the thought may occur to you, "How do they do that? It's so far outside of my abilities." Quite simply they acquired skills through the process of setting a goal, putting a plan in place, and practicing with the right attitude and proper instruction. They integrated their body, mind, and spirit; developed virtuous habits; and persevered. They followed a variation of the same map I am offering to you.

The internal skills developed through perseverance and a focus on self-actualization can be just as impressive. You may not get a standing ovation for a small act of mindfulness but it is impressive to notice in someone or experience yourself. I am occasionally asked how I am able to bring a calm, rational mindset to difficult situations. Believe me, it's a learned skill. I was a hypercompetitive young person. It served me well in some ways and was a detriment in others. I achieved some success, but my inner self could become unduly judgmental and dismissive of myself and others. I put more focus on developing skills that society seemed to deem important: competing, winning, acquiring, self-involvement. Compassion, reflection, and gratitude were distant concepts and served no real purpose to my younger self. Maybe this is just a function of the growing up and becoming wiser that most of us go through, but many of us never really leave the immature mindset behind. And others seem to figure things out at a young age and never look back.

No matter where you are on the spectrum, now is a good time to up your game. As you read these words, there will no doubt be some crisis (or crises) in progress affecting your life on a personal or global level. This is exactly the right time to use or develop the skills that help navigate any difficult situation. Meditation and focused breathing can help calm you and return you to the present moment. Healthy eating and exercise can feed your physical self that needs nourishing. Embracing challenge and showing kindness enable you to cope and care for others.

When you react to difficult times with perseverance and focus on the things that matter, you are making the best of whatever arises. This is the silver lining—the personal growth and mutual uplifting that can transmute crisis into opportunity.

Michael Jordan didn't make his high school varsity basketball team on his first try. He was relegated to junior varsity.

Albert Einstein was a slow learner. His parents and teachers thought he had learning disabilities.

Walt Disney was fired from his first job because his cartoons weren't creative enough.

Elvis Presley was kicked out of the Grand Ole Opry after his first show and told to go back to driving a truck.

Oprah Winfrey was fired from her first job as evening news reporter, reportedly being told she was "unfit for television news."

I have never met anyone who didn't have setbacks in their life. In fact, it's the setbacks that set the stage for the comebacks. Perseverance is one of the most admirable human qualities. If you want to start a good conversation with someone successful, ask them to share their failures. If you are going through a tough time, remember that you're not alone. Find someone you can count on to listen, lift your spirits, and make you smile. Remember to pause and take a deep breath. Hang in there, keep trying, and ask others for help along the way, because we all root for the underdog.

LUCK

So we do all the right things. We work hard, treat our body and others well, and make the world a better place. Then we get hit by the cancer bus, or a real bus. Life isn't fair.

By sheer accident of place and time of birth, our economic and social prospects are largely determined. If you were a young able man of fighting age during the many wars of the twentieth century, your chances for survival or escaping without mental health issues were dismal. Born in Bangladesh to peasant farmers? Good luck getting that corner office. Severe physical defects? No pickleball for you.

Even on a less existential level, your choice of a career and a spouse were largely the result of luck. What caused you to head down a vocational path or find your soul mate? Accidents of geography, circumstance, and genetics have shaped our lives far more than we often admit. I have to shake my head at the guy who says, "I did this on my own. I'm a self-made man." None of us do anything on our own. We can't even lay claim to most of our own thoughts on some level. They are the product of neural pathways and psychological traits that took shape before we went to kindergarten. Without the support of others, the right social, political and religious climate, rule of law, and, yes, dumb luck, any of us could have landed anywhere on the spectrum.

I'm willing to take credit for hard work and developing skills that took me where I wanted to go. But nobody does it on their own. I was *really* lucky to be born to caring parents in a free country during a time when I didn't have to go to war. I didn't get sick, my brain worked even before my common sense kicked in, and my internal programming was usually optimistic.

When I speak with successful business people who are decent human beings I am struck by their acknowledgment of the role luck has played in their lives. Many of these entrepreneurs have failed, sometimes spectacularly. But something in their genetic wiring and brain chemistry caused them to keep trying and searching. They managed to run into the right people at the right time. They stayed healthy. They worked hard. But they also got lucky.

I know full well what it is to be lucky. A cellular mutation, a drunk driver, or a random accident could have derailed my story at any moment in the past. And, of course, anything could happen in the future to me or my loved ones. All I can do is enjoy the good fortune I have had to this point and continue to try to lead a life well lived. A big part of that life is paying it forward. Luck has not been as kind to others through no fault of their own so I continue to seek to ease suffering as I can.

The takeaway is that a little humility and gratitude are in order. Our very existence has been made possible by a countless series of successful reproduction events against all odds from the beginning of life on our planet. So many people have given us love and support, starting with our parents and including teachers, mentors, and friends.

Some compassion is in order too. It's easy to lay blame at the feet of the poor or immigrant populations for our social problems. But they are often just fellow participants in the luck lottery, born or fallen into circumstances that might have crushed any one of us. When we care for others who are less fortunate and give with a sense of humility, we acknowledge our own good fortune.

FINDING YOU *HAVE* ENOUGH

> "It is not the man who has too little, but the man who craves more, that is poor."
>
> – *Seneca*

How much is enough? Consumerism has become a way of life that is tilted in favor of the producers rather than the end users. Everywhere you go in the real world, but especially online and on TV, you are bombarded with ads that have become much more sophisticated, tracking your clicks to see what items are being searched for and what topics hold your interest. The overriding message is that you do not have enough or, more insidiously, that you are not enough. Content people don't feel an urgent need to buy things. They are more likely to make purchases based on legitimate needs rather than unexamined whims, so if this book brings you greater contentment, you'll also be saving money: Happiness and wealth in one handy book. Such a deal!

Living within your means, the feeling of self-control, and realizing that things are impermanent can lead to much greater satisfaction than indulging every want. As Matthew Kelly asks in *The Rhythm of Life*—are you caught up in incessant wanting rather than feeling satisfied with meeting your legitimate needs? Time with friends and family will matter more in the big scheme of things than your possessions. You don't see many obituaries that instead of "beloved wife and mother" read "former owner of a new BMW and seventy pairs of shoes."

A good friend's father recently died and my friend told me he had spent the morning taking his dad's personal items and either throwing them away or putting them in boxes. We agreed that it may sound trite, but experiences and time spent together were the only real things that mattered. Our times on the court are a perfect example of savoring enjoyment and connection rather than acquisition and consumption. Give me a paddle, a ball, and some friends: What more do you need? Align your focus with what really matters and become the architect of a simpler, truly richer life.

THE IMPORTANCE OF REVIEW

As a lifelong learner and occasional teacher, I have a great appreciation for the process of review. Transferring important information from short-term to long-term memory requires that we go back and check in on the things we want to keep uppermost in our minds. I keep my favorite books in one section of a bookcase in my home. When I feel the urge I will walk over and pick out a book and go over the highlights I have made in the text. Often I will be encouraged to find that I am implementing this found wisdom. I can also become inspired once again to explore interesting subjects and discover what new meanings they now might hold for me.

Reviewing my pickleball journal, I am reminded of the principles that bring out my best game and the stories that always make me smile. When I pull up pictures on my devices, memories are stirred that generate a range of positive emotions. The process of review improves memory and performance and reminds you of what's important.

I encourage you to highlight this book when you find something that resonates with you. Become an active participant in this process we call life. Write it down in your "action plan" or anywhere else that keeps it fresh in your mind. Remember the power of review and the act of writing—it can make the difference between idle contemplation and active implementation.

ACTION PLAN, SECTION 2

In this section of your journal, describe how you currently feel about your relationship with challenge and your willingness to embrace change. Assess your level of discipline. It's likely that you are disciplined in some ways and not in others. Explore if your discipline in specific areas correlates with success or happiness.

How do I typically face challenges?

____

____

____

Do I like change?

____

____

____

Are there areas where I could be more disciplined?

____

____

____

What do you want to learn in the coming year? Job skills? A new language? A solid third-shot drive? Financial literacy? How will you go about doing it? Reading, online courses, or personalized instruction?

____

____

____

Consider talking to friends and see what directions they have taken to feed their minds. Write down your goals and your strategies. And remember to actively review your game plan. When you prioritize learning, it not only becomes a source of personal improvement, but another source of entertainment. Learning is FUNdamental! (Sorry. I went there.)

REST STOP

I have fond memories of taking road trips with my family when I was younger. Our longest trip was in our old Ford pickup with the camper shell as we made our way from Panama to North Carolina through Central America. The scenery was amazing but I remember the odd things best, like when the border guards in Costa Rica took our spare tire because they said it might have yellow fever mosquitos inside of it. Judging by their collection, I'm sure the guys ran a thriving tire business down the road. What impressed me most was my father's sudden command of the profane aspects of the Spanish language, which I had never heard him use before.

He was also an avid photographer and decided to give us boys a couple of cameras to get our artistic view of the stunning vistas and human stories along the way. He seemed somewhat disappointed upon our return to come back from the photo store (remember those?) and find about 200 pictures of...cows.

There were long hours on the highway at times but the feeling of going somewhere was always exciting. I hope you've enjoyed *our* journey so far but even the dog's legs are crossed by now, and it's time to pull over at the next rest stop, stretch our legs, and look up at the amazing sky. Taking a break to reenergize gives us renewed focus to continue on our way. After all, we've covered a lot of ground. We have explored the following:

- **Rationality and Habits**

  We are not rational beings. We are rationalizing beings. Virtuous habits and a rational plan facilitate meaningful change.

- **Mindset**

  A growth mindset is the key to seeing life as an opportunity instead of a threat.

- **Hardwiring Happiness**

  Overcome your negative bias by giving much more attention to positive aspects of your life.

- **Pickleball Lessons**

  Skill matters. Gratitude, relationships and fun matter more. Work hard, play hard, but above all, "carpe dink-em": seize the joy every day you get to play a game with your friends.

- **Perspective**

  We don't see things as they are, we see them as we are. Don't take things personally, give more than you take, and watch life open up before you.

- **Awareness and Competence**

  Developing awareness sets the stage for the journey from ignorance to unconscious competence where you play in an optimal state of flow.

- **Emotional Intelligence**

  Develop "E.I." and live in harmony with others — peaceful, accepting and content.

- **Finding Enough**
  When you are enough, you don't need anyone or anything to complete you—they merely enrich your life.

- **Building a Physical Foundation**
  Eat well. Move more. Repeat.

We have also discussed subjects that impact our quest to integrate our mind, heart, and spirit, such as:

- **Life Skills**
  Employ your growth mindset to develop new life skills. Reconnect with your natural love of learning.

- **Your Relationship to Challenge, Change, and Discipline**
  Embracing these concepts frees you to live more dynamically and less fearfully. Lean into life and feel the power of actively creating your best self.

- **Perseverance**
  Hang in there, my friend. When you keep trying, you honor your journey and accept the outcome with head held high.

Take a couple of additional minutes to contemplate the importance of any of the above subjects that speaks to you at this moment and consider how you might focus on them moving forward. If you can make progress in any of these categories, I guarantee you will get more out of the big pickleball game of life.

MANAGING EMOTIONS

> "No one cares how much you know, until they know how much you care."
>
> – *Theodore Roosevelt*

DO YOU EVER FEEL THAT YOU KNOW the right action to take on an intellectual level but it just doesn't seem that you apply it consistently enough? Emotions are incredibly powerful and can short-circuit wise action. In fact, in the brain, emotion precedes thought; every thought and every action is launched from an emotional origin. Much of what constitutes maturity and wisdom is recognizing our emotional underpinnings—and then taking rational action. We cannot change our thinking and make emotions go away. Only when we learn to observe hidden emotions can we begin the process of *acting* from our higher self rather than *reacting* based on pure emotion.

Observing a young child can be very informative. They haven't developed the filters necessary to translate emotion into wise action.

"Mine!"
"Gimme!"
"No fair!"
"I'm afraid!"
"WAAAAHHHHH!"

Actually, you may know adults and fellow players who still act on this level. They may not throw tantrums (okay, maybe some do) but their emotions still scream these messages with only a veneer of civility.

"Mine!" and "Gimme!" become a fixation on consumerism to placate a deep emotion of desire. Or they can be the basis of a jealous, possessive attitude toward relationships. "No fair!" becomes a nonacceptance of reality and a sense of victimhood (especially when several shots in a row hit the tape and fall on your side of the net). "I'm afraid!" can evolve into a fear of failure and change. And screaming and crying often translate into habitual complaining or the inability to accept line calls and move beyond emotion to solve problems.

A variation on the "Four Stages of Competence" I discussed earlier, there are four stages on the "Road to Emotional Awareness":

- **STAGE ONE** is complete unawareness.
- **STAGE TWO** is developing awareness after the fact and trying to do better next time.
- **STAGE THREE** is recognizing unhealthy behaviors as they are happening. This can be a particularly tough stage because it's like witnessing yourself spiraling out of control while feeling helpless to stop it.

- **STAGE FOUR** is recognizing emotions before they do unnecessary harm to yourself and others. Only then can you act from a higher place and learn to deal with yourself and others in the healthiest way possible. Stage Four is a happy place indeed. It is like channeling great wisdom and consistently shining its light out into the world. Regardless of circumstance, it is peaceful, loving, and understanding.

One trap that can lie in wait for you is denying emotions. There is a huge chasm between recognition and denial. Emotions are a part of every one of us. It's literally how our brains are wired—emotion precedes thought. Denying emotions is unrealistic and can result in an unhealthy suppression of feelings that need to be constructively expressed. Seeing emotions for what they are reduces the power they have over you without pretending they don't matter. The key is to engage your wise self to not deny, but manage the flow of naturally arising emotions.

I'm suspicious of those who claim to be free of the pull of emotions—okay, maybe jealous is a better world. But unless you have any Vulcans in your family tree, chances are that you're just like me and most everyone else. What really gets you? Politics? Traffic? Rude people? Financial stress? Dinking easy balls into the net? Identify your personal minefields so you can apply the stages of dealing effectively with the interplay of emotion and rationality.

CONNECTION: FEEDING YOUR HEART

Studies show that people who feel lonely or depressed are three to ten times more likely to get sick and die prematurely. The health insurer Cigna, found a nearly 13 percent rise in loneliness since 2018. Their survey found 63 percent of men to be lonely, compared with 58 percent of women. Social media use was tied to loneliness as well, with 73 percent of very heavy social media users considered lonely, as compared with 52 percent of light users.[1]

It's hard to overstate this problem. Why has loneliness become so prevalent? And how can we fight it?

There are many reasons why we have grown apart as a society. Technology may be a primary culprit. We are not so gradually limiting real human contact in the workplace and among friends, yet we have a deep tribal need to connect. For millennia our social units have been based on intimate group dynamics with the family, workplace, and community serving as touchstones and providing a sense of belonging. Today interpersonal communication has fragmented and become a pale shadow of the formerly rich interplay between people. We used to visit friends to talk. Then we used to call friends on the phone. Now we text or email without the benefits of inflection, nuance, and eye contact. A good conversation has become so valuable because it is so rare.

People can be messy. They can be hard to connect with because they have built up the same defense mechanisms that we all have. It feels bad to get hurt or be thought of in a negative way, so we often isolate ourselves where it's safe. But as the statistics above show, alone is the most dangerous place you can be. So what can be done?

[1] Renken, Elena. "Most Americans Are Lonely, And Our Workplace Culture May Not Be Helping." NPR. NPR, January 23, 2020. https://www.npr.org/sections/health-shots/2020/01/23/798676465/most-americans-are-lonely-and-our-workplace-culture-may-not-be-helping.

Get Out There

Hit the court, find a club. Pickleball is a great antidote to isolation; its social nature encourages connection. I was surprised when I put together the list of invitees to my sixtieth birthday party. A substantial number of guests had a pickleball connection. My longtime friends were in attendance of course, but it was gratifying to see that enough connections had been made on the court to justify spending one of my best days with my pickleball posse. There is joy in belonging and pickleball is a fun way to find that feeling. Connect with those who are receptive and try not to take it personally if others are not. Just one good friend can make all the difference in your life. Just three good friends and it's game on!

Reconnect

If you are in a committed relationship, it might be worthwhile to have a talk that lets your partner know you value them and want to reinvigorate certain aspects of your lives together. Suggest something that gives you shared time, such as taking walks together to improve your health and provide time free from distractions that promotes good conversation. Read and discuss books or watch a show that is thought-provoking and spurs discussion. (Maybe something on PBS rather than *Real Housewives*, but hey . . . you do you.) Do home projects that promote teamwork and creative thinking. Make time for travel, date nights, concerts, or anything else that you enjoy that might have been pushed aside over time.

If you have a friend that you haven't seen for a while, reach out and find time for coffee or some other activity. Sometimes friendships need a little jump start to get them going again.

Get a Pet

Our new guy, Cabo. Say "Awww..."

There's something irrational about finding an animal and devoting time, money, and attention to it, cleaning up after it, feeding it, and planning your schedule around its needs. But if you feel lonely or people don't seem to be doing the trick, it is completely rational to get a pet. Petting or even making eye contact with a pet produces endorphins and stress-reducing chemicals in the body. I'm a dog person but find what works for you. Dogs are one of the great sources of unconditional love on offer. They can be an example of bliss on four legs. As the joke goes, my spouse never seems to run out of the garage, jump around, and lick my face when I come home. But the next time you need a laugh, feel free to visualize that actually happening. At the very least, it would startle your neighbors.

Travel

Traveling gets us out of our routine and helps us to really notice and become more present. It can be life-affirming to see other cultures that may have different levels of wealth or "exotic" customs and food, but have the same basic desires to be loved, connect, and laugh together. Our level of compassion can be enhanced when we find the common bonds among people throughout the world who are often divided from us only by politics, culture, and religion. When we find each other's humanity and see that we are all in this together, feelings arise that promote connection in a deep and meaningful way.

It's also great to connect with fellow travelers. There is something about being literally on the same journey together that promotes communication and shared stories. My wife and I recently got seated with a couple from Brazil on a cruise and though we could barely communicate, we were able to get points across and from the laughter arising at our table, people around us would have thought we were lifelong friends.

Be Kind

Connect through kindness. Kindness can be as simple as sharing a smile and a nod or as deep as helping someone through a life trauma. A sincere compliment or acknowledgment can powerfully affect someone's mood. Allowing a car to cut into traffic or holding open a door for a stranger makes almost no impact on your day but can brighten someone else's mood.

When I have had the opportunity to emcee charity events, I have sometimes touched on what I call the selfishness of giving. Yes, giving freely of your time, treasure, or talent sets off all kinds of immunity-boosting, endorphin-releasing, parasympathetic nervous system-enhancing reactions in you. Embrace it! This is actually a classic win-win scenario. So give. Be kind. You never know how far your kindness will travel and how many lives it will touch.

TEMPER TEMPER

Your emotions are powerful—powerful enough to short-circuit any improvements to your well-being. As with the mind, the mere act of observing emotions can sap them of their power over you. Next time you miss an easy shot and get mad, take a mental step back and feel what it's like to be angry—the tightness, the rush of blood to the head, the exclusion of everything else around you. Observe the sensations, then decide how long you want to stay angry. What purpose does it serve? Does the state of anger solve anything? If not, let the emotion run through you and proceed as soon as possible to finding wise solutions. What can you do to change the situation for the better? Maybe all you can do is accept what you can't change and get on with your day. Either way, you strip the emotion of its control over you and you take back the reins of your mental state.

In *My Stroke of Insight*, Dr. Jill Bolte Taylor describes her ordeal of dealing with the effects of a stroke that severely damaged the left hemisphere of her brain. It's a riveting story, but one thing I remember in particular is how she learned to deal with anger after experiencing the sensation of how her healthy right brain observed the actions taking place in her recovering left brain.

She now allows her left brain to throw a tantrum when something bad happens but it only gets one minute or so to silently scream, hold its breath, and drop some "F bombs." It is this stepping apart that brings the right brain into play. It becomes the witness to the pain. It holds that fearful, angry part of you in a tender embrace and allows the healing to begin. When the minute is up, you can take a deep breath and get right back to the task at hand of managing the situation calmly and rationally.

This same process can ease other unhealthy states such as worry, guilt, shame, and fear. Turn the flashlight onto the emotion. See it for what it is … a passing state, a temporary phenomenon. The reason we are not rational is because we get carried away with emotion, sometimes to the extent that emotion becomes the biggest part of who we are. Learn to observe and realize that you are more than your emotions. They are just a part of your circuitry. You have the power to put them in their place—but it takes practice.

PRACTICE

> "What are we talkin' about? We talkin' about practice, man."
>
> *–Allen Iverson*

In NBA star Allen Iverson's epic and humorous rant about practice, he stumbles on some important things. In one breath, he allows "I know it's important" before going on to mock the idea of practicing at length. But at the time, he was a basketball guru; he had attained hoop enlightenment. Before he got there I guarantee you he spent countless hours practicing, honing his skills so that he could skillfully respond to whatever was thrown at him on the court.

When someone tells me that it's hard to meditate and observe thoughts and emotions, I completely agree with them. It's one of the hardest things you can do. That's why they call it a spiritual *practice*. Malcolm Gladwell writes eloquently about the ten thousand-hour rule: the idea that it takes ten thousand hours of practice to approach mastery at anything. You may not have ten thousand hours available to sit on a cushion in the lotus position and unlock the secrets of the universe. But if the goal is experiencing some peace and understanding rather than vibrating out of existence, give it a shot. As with any pursuit, it's about finding the place where discovery and learning happen in a place of enjoyment.

Practice is closely related to discipline, which we discussed earlier. They both have negative connotations for many of us, but that's just your emotional self throwing a hissy fit. Your higher self is patiently waiting to be called off the bench and put in the game. Your pickleball game gets better with focused practice. If you also train other aspects of yourself you will be ready to excel when it's game time.

FEAR

In *The Untethered Soul*, Michael Singer describes how fear is the basis of self-consciousness, insecurity, and anxiety:

> Stop for a moment and see what you have given your mind to do. You said to your mind, "I want everyone to like me. I don't want anyone to speak badly of me. I want everything I say and do to be acceptable and pleasing to everyone. I don't want anyone to hurt me. I don't want anything to happen that I don't like. And I want everything to happen that I do like." Then you said, "Now mind, figure out how to make every one of these things a reality, even if you have to think about it day and night." And of course your mind said, "I'm on the job. I will work on it constantly."[2]

It's little wonder we can be a mental and emotional mess. We have taken on the impossible task to please our psyche and make everything okay. Our emotions are triggered when we find this isn't so. We become afraid of being found out for who we really are. We fear the future.

[2] Michael A. Singer, "Chapter 10," in *The Untethered Soul: The Journey Beyond Yourself* (Oakland, CA: New Harbinger Publications, Inc., 2013), p. 91.

We strive to control a random world so that we never feel pain. Only when we realize that our task is impossible can we relax and do what is within our reach.

You can actually shine the light on your mind trying to make everything perfect and smile at the absurdity of it all—the folly of trying to take an unpredictable world and make it conform to your will. Please do this now. Literally, please stop right now and take a minute to realize the impossibility of what you have been trying to do your whole life.

Interesting, eh? This realization can help ease the urge to control the uncontrollable. Most of us never take this simple step. We never let ourselves off the hook for not being perfect or as good as someone else—for not being enough. We need to acknowledge that everyone is in the same boat and get on with the more manageable task of finding balance instead of perfection.

I sometimes laugh at my fear by picturing the gag from *Wayne's World* where Wayne and Garth bow down on the floor in front of one of their heroes and exclaim, "We're not worthy! We're not worthy!" The feeling of unworthiness is comical when two grungy dudes are having fun with the idea. But unworthiness is at the heart of our personal fears. On some level, we fear that if someone really knew us, they wouldn't love us.

Everyone works hard to broadcast an image of themselves into the world. That image can be brilliant, nurturing, enlightened, successful, pickleball savant, etc... The problem is that many of us don't really believe it. It may help to realize that everyone is playing the same game to some degree. There may be personal qualities of which we are rightly proud, but the pressure to be everything to everyone can be exhausting.

We cannot escape our fears; they serve the vital purpose of keeping us safe from real and present dangers until the point when they haunt and dominate our lives. Seeing the futility of what we have asked our minds to do is a useful process to understand why mental and emotional issues can arise. Once we see the process we can begin to come to grips with the way fear works. Fear lives in all of us. Only when we pause and learn to observe it are we empowered to make courageous choices to build the lives we want.

WHY WORRY?

> "Worrying does not take away tomorrow's troubles. It takes away today's peace."
>
> – *Randy Armstrong*

Fear lives in the space between reality and possibility. Worry inhabits the same realm; it's merely fear of the future experienced in the present moment. "What might happen?" "What will people think of me if I fail (miss that shot)?" As Mark Twain said, "Some of the worst things in my life never even happened." Worrying accomplishes nothing; preparation and building your skillset are concrete steps that enable you to meet the future at your best.

One way to disarm worry and anxiety is to step back from the swirl of future possibilities and ask yourself, "What can I do right now?" If appropriate, take action. If there is nothing to be done, try to accept that truth and become fully engaged in the only place you can make a difference: the present moment. Feel gratitude for whatever good things you are currently experiencing. Your mind will want to continue to work on the problem but remember that this is the job of the mind. See your own mind with compassion. Maybe give it a virtual hug and a pat on the head. "*Shhh . . .*"

THE COMPARISON TRAP

We are constantly making comparisons: Is this better than that? Is he (or she) better than me at [INSERT ACTIVITY HERE]? It can be an emotional minefield when the comparisons involve your self-image. Comparison to others in your family, peer group, or social media contacts deeply affects your sense of status and happiness. Social media, because of its curated nature, can be particularly damaging in this regard. Fear of missing out (FOMO) and the highlight reel quality of many posts leave a feeling of not measuring up, experientially and personally. (Maybe it's time to unfriend skinny Samantha and her nonstop series of perfect yoga poses on sunlit cliffs in the Italian Riviera.)

So much of our happiness is dictated by our surroundings and with whom we associate. I touched on this concept when discussing the role of the comparison trap as it applies to your pickleball experience. If you have solid pickleball skills but always compete in games with 5.0 players, you can feel less than by comparison. You might have a nice house but if you live in a neighborhood where your home is smaller and has fewer bells and whistles than your neighbor's, you might feel a sense of lacking rather than contentment. From physical appearance to job status to athletic ability, it can be difficult to feel that you're enough on some level.

One can also fall victim to self-comparison: "I used to be so thin, young, vibrant, sharp, sexual, important . . . " Plastic surgeons, therapists, and purveyors of magic pills do a brisk business taking care of this mindset. Understanding this syndrome is at the center of finding you're enough. Feeling "less than" is a difficult way to live. Companies and their ad agencies are only too willing to point out that you don't have enough and you are not enough. "But if you only had this Mercedes, this deodorant, or that jacket . . . " The only real solution is to bring your focus back to yourself. Once you make the game about *your* journey, you are actually doing something within your control.

Take a minute to see where this is happening in your life. Is it happening in your pickleball game? Are you suffering because of something real or is a mental comparison to someone else or your past dictating your happiness? Do you need to acquire something to make you happy or is that something already within you? Are you resisting the truth of your aging to the point that no matter what positive steps you take, you are left feeling despondent or helpless? Whether the comparisons are external or internal, bringing them into awareness can reduce the power they have over you.

You can't control how good a player John is or how much money Jean makes, so why waste psychic energy comparing yourself. Good for them! Respect the attributes of others whether they are subjectively better or worse than you. Then get back to work on being the best that *you* can be. That's the only game worth playing.

GREAT EXPECTATIONS

Another obstacle that can undermine our happiness is unrealistic expectations. Author and historian Yuval Harari explains, "Happiness depends on expectations rather than objective conditions. We don't become satisfied by leading a peaceful and prosperous existence. Rather, we become satisfied when reality matches our expectations. The bad news is that as conditions improve, expectations balloon."[3]

Expectations can sabotage your pickleball experience. You may improve some skills but what you did well yesterday may elude you

[3] Yuval N. Harari, *Homo Deus: A Brief History of Tomorrow* (New York, NY: Harper Perennial, 2018).

today. Your body may be willing on some days but your mind may be on holiday, or vice versa. Unrealistic expectations can make a fun game an exercise in frustration or make a wonderful life seem unfulfilling and empty.

The process of improvement and awareness we discussed previously can give you a real opportunity to improve your game and make positive change in your life. But don't expect fireworks. You may make huge breakthroughs and discoveries on this journey, but don't expect everyone to fall at your feet in worship at the new you. Outward change can be noticeable but inner change is more subtle. It's vastly more important that *you* know the effort you have put in and that the moments of contentment and realization that have infused your life are completely worthwhile.

Having goals is recommended but those goals should be reasonable. It is essential to manage expectations. If you find that you are easily disappointed with your pickleball game, people, or life, take a step back and see if your expectations are realistic. It's an imperfect world. Sometimes things don't work out as you would like. What did you expect?

THE IDIOT FACTOR

Sometimes we can expect too much of others. Some folks may have a life history we can't see that has trapped them in unhealthy behaviors. Compassion is a wise first step when dealing with difficult people. Life is hard. By all means, reach out to those who need a little extra attention and patience. But at some point, you need to draw the line on unacceptable behavior. Sometimes you just have to walk (or run) the other way.

There are roughly 10 percent of us (trying to be nice here ...) who on any given day qualify as idiots. These percentages may increase during political campaigns, rush hour traffic, and tournament play.

You know who they are. They cut you off in traffic, berate waiters, run countries, "miss" line calls, write "pickleball enlightenment" books …

The problem is we are hardwired to notice and dwell on the bad actors. The pleasant, somewhat well-adjusted masses glide quietly under our radar but when the idiot rears his ugly head, everyone notices. In the world of business, politics, sports, and entertainment, idiots are particularly visible by using their position to create an outsized, and often negative, impact on society.

You are the filter through which everything else is experienced, so it might be a good idea to give that idiot filter a little cleaning and maintenance. A rational defense against idiocy is to take a deep breath and simply shift your focus. Don't give the idiots the attention they crave and allow them to poison your view of humanity. Resist the urge to be like a moth flying toward the flame; instead, surround yourself with people who lift you up rather than bring you down. Let the idiots make their noise. By all means, oppose them when you must, but when you can't, turn your focus to the 90 percent of the world (still staying positive!) that makes you glad to be a part of it. Life is too short to let the idiots hijack your happiness.

RELATIONSHIPS

We are constantly managing a myriad of relationships. Spouses, friends, family, coworkers, neighbors and our very selves demand attention and require a range of skills to negotiate appropriately. There are many sayings which get to the heart of the importance of good relationships. And then there are these:

> "Before you marry a person you should first make them use a computer with slow internet to see who they really are."
>
> – *Will Ferrell*

"My wife and I were really happy for twenty years. Then we met."

– *Rodney Dangerfield*

"My neighbor's diary says that I have boundary issues."

– *Mini Tantrums*

The quality of our relationships correlates strongly with the quality of our lives. We are social creatures and how we relate to those closest to us is crucial to our well-being. So how do we develop strong relationships, learn to trust, and let others into our lives in meaningful ways? We can start with heeding the words of Don Miguel Ruiz, author of *The Four Agreements*. These agreements apply to a range of subjects but I find that they are particularly useful when applied to relationships.

Agreement #1: Be impeccable with your word.

Speak with integrity. Say what you mean. Don't speak against yourself or gossip about others. Use the power of your word in the direction of truth and love.

Agreement #2: Don't take anything personally.

Nothing others do is because of you. It's a projection of their own reality. You will reduce your suffering when you learn this truth.

Agreement #3: Don't make assumptions.

Ask questions and express what you really want. Communicate clearly to avoid misunderstandings and drama.

Agreement #4: Always do your best.

> Your best will vary from moment to moment. Doing your best will help you to avoid self-judgment and regret.

To sum up, say what you mean in a loving way, clearly express what you want, don't take things personally, and do your best—pretty simple and straightforward, but powerful as well.

The Golden Rule is another oldie but goodie when it comes to relationship dynamics. "Treat others as you wish to be treated" could solve a lot of dysfunctional relationships. The Golden Rule has a lot to do with respect—and mutual respect is one of the strongest indicators of relationship health among family, spouses, and friends.

CURATING YOUR RELATIONSHIPS

When we curate relationships we actively select the people with whom we want to spend time and share our lives. This applies in spades to our pickleball partners. Who lifts you up or brings you down? Who cares about what you have to say and treats you with respect? Who is just flat out fun?

You might be related to someone or care deeply about them but that doesn't mean you have to spend time with them other than what is required by circumstance. We have some friends for life. There are other people with whom we are thrown together by family, work, or extended social circles. When this happens, some curation might be in order.

Obviously, people don't all fit seamlessly together. That would be great for world peace but it's never going to happen, not even in relatively small groups. This is when we might consider limiting our contact with those who have values or behaviors that don't sync with ours. In some cases we need to completely remove ourselves from a relationship. It's not necessary to tell someone off and blab about it to everyone else in the group—this is a pragmatic decision and doesn't need to devolve into confrontation and histrionics. Make the process as simple as possible. If you get pushback or antagonism from the other party, details are best left unsaid if possible. Explain that you just don't mesh together that well for whatever reason and let it go at that.

At other times it's just easier and better to limit contact when possible. Find ways to avoid situations where you are thrown together. If you *are* together seek to be as nonreactive as possible. Often we have trouble with people who push our buttons and want a reaction. When we don't give it to them we take away their confrontational energy. They don't get the drama they want and eventually move on to greener pastures.

Sometimes we don't need to curate our friends. We need to curate our conversations. Many of my friends know where I stand on certain hot-button topics and I know where they stand. This extends to views on religion, politics, climate change, or immigration policies. Most friends know better than to intentionally antagonize each other. Really good friends can still discuss anything and laugh about it later. Either way we constantly have opportunities to improve the quality of our lives. It's up to us to consciously decide with whom and what we surround ourselves.

A SINCERE COMPLIMENT

If you really want to surprise someone, give them a sincere compliment. They are as rare as they are wonderful. Imagine somebody taking the time to notice you and even fit some praise for you into their busy schedule. Ideally we don't do good things in search of admiration, but a little love and respect thrown our way can brighten our day and encourage us to do even better. It's also a great boost when someone notices some personal quality or aspect of your game that you have been working on improving. If there is someone in your life who you might be taking for granted, find some way to look them in the eyes and compliment them on something simple: "Your hair looks great today!" "Nice shot!" Or as my wife tells me, "You sure married well!"

It's also good to know how to take a compliment. I used to habitually deflect compliments and feel generally uncomfortable receiving them. I have since learned to reply with a heartfelt, "Thank you. I really appreciate you saying that." Or something to that effect. And if it feels natural, give a compliment in kind: "Yes, I *am* an amazing player. That's perceptive of you to notice how wonderful and incredible I am."

A compliment isn't as complicated as some of the other topics discussed in this section. But it's a direct path to someone's heart.

ACCEPTANCE AND UNDERSTANDING

It's important to try and understand. But when it comes to people it's usually better to accept. Let's face it; it's hard enough to understand yourself much less your spouse or your pickleball partner. Understanding behaviors is next to impossible. Psychologists still haven't completely figured out what makes us tick. Is your friend sincere or is she just "virtue signaling" to achieve some other goal? Why does your partner hit crappy lobs when you're standing at the kitchen line? How can your uncle still be a Chargers fan after they left him for Los Angeles?

I tend to be a little OCD and my wife likes to leave things out so they are easier to find that afternoon or next September. We didn't go to marriage counseling to figure out why the other one is terribly wrong. We worked out a way to live together and accept our differences that keeps us both relatively happy.

One coping mechanism I have used when looking back at failures or personal conflict is to realize that I and the others involved only knew what we knew then. This doesn't apply only to a lack of information but to a number of things, including personal history, inexperience, or immaturity. Again, seek to understand but accept what happened. Acceptance is the starting point to getting back on track again whether it involves something as trivial as mistakes on the court or as serious as dealing with the death of a loved one.

One of the most profound things we can do is to accept ourselves and others; to not turn away and refuse to see, but accept with eyes wide open. If what we see is destructive or dangerous behavior, then we remove ourselves from a thoroughly unacceptable situation. Otherwise, we see the situation with clarity and take action from a place of acceptance rather than denial.

This is how we learn to cope in an uncertain world without enough information to understand why we do what we do and why we are here in the first place. Self-acceptance is the first step. Once we make headway on that front, it's so much easier to accept others. When love is predicated on understanding, love is conditional. Acceptance is unconditional. It is one of the greatest gifts we can give to others—and ourselves.

ACTION PLAN, PART 3

Write down the emotional states you enjoy the most. What makes your heart sing? Concerts, pickleball, dinners with friends, carefree time with your loved ones? Make it a point to schedule what you enjoy most. Describe times when you felt loved or accepted. What internal feelings do you savor the most? What and who makes you feel satisfied, proud, useful, appreciated?

____

____

____

____

____

Now list the emotional states that get in your way more than others. Is it worry, guilt, anxiety, fear? (All of the above? Put down the journal and have a glass of wine or three.) Focus on one aspect and write down steps you can take when the feeling arises. If it's worry, focus on the Serenity Prayer. If you keep falling into the same traps on the court of negative self-talk, anger, or nonacceptance, write down what it feels like, make a plan to observe it, and give yourself positive feedback when you are able to manage your emotions in a positive way. Work to forgive yourself for what you were unable to control in the past and write down what you have learned to prevent future occurrences. Apologize and make amends when possible.

____

____

____

____

____

Write down specific ways you would like to increase your connection if desired. Explore areas of your life in which you fall into the comparison trap and shift your focus back to yourself, celebrating your own abilities and progress. Examine your relationships and write down what aspects you would like to improve. Communication? Intimacy? Time spent together?

____

____

____

____

____

____

____

Record an instance when you gave a sincere compliment and describe the reaction from the other person and how you felt doing it. Meditate on how it feels when you are practicing acceptance. Describe the sensations. Are you more peaceful? Do you spend less time complaining and more time being present?

____

____

____

____

____

____

____

Observing your emotions in writing can be instructive. When you bring them to light in this way, their power to lift you up can be inspiring and their power to hurt you can diminish. Describe your progress as you become more aware of the way your emotions shape your life.

___

___

___

___

___

___

When our body, mind, and heart are working in concert, life is beautiful. We feel good, achieve more, and live with an openness and lightness of heart that enables us to connect with others. Every day isn't perfect but we learn to smooth out the rough spots and engage with life at our best. This is what it feels like to live well.

Now we are ready to take it to the next level; to savor this amazing life and imbue it with meaning and purpose.

OBSERVING THE MIND

"When you run after your thoughts, you are like a dog chasing a stick: every time a stick is thrown, you run after it. Instead, be like a lion who, rather than chasing after the stick, turns to face the thrower. One only throws a stick at a lion once."

– *Jetsun Milarepa*

The quote above can mean two things. One, it is better to examine and face your thoughts than to run around wildly after them. Or two, don't throw sticks at lions. (Seriously. What are you thinking? They will mess you up.)

What do you say when someone asks, "What is most important to you?" I know it's pickleball but let's pretend there's are other worthwhile things in life. Chances are it's some variation on health, friends, family, happiness, and security. Only when you know yourself better can you experience more health, wealth, and harmony. To do that you need the right information and the right mindset. But everything depends on *you*. So you might as well get to know you a little better.

You are a complicated creature, arguably the most outstanding product ever produced by evolution. Take a bow! When we pull together toward noble goals, become mindful of our actions, and hold values that are rooted in kindness and mutual prosperity, beautiful things happen. However, when we become fragmented and overly tribal, no other species can match our ability to screw things up on a global level. We fear not having or being enough so we compensate by taking more than we need by any means necessary. If we look at life as a zero-sum game and see others as threats, then selfishness and violence produce a tragic world.

Basically, there is a race underway. Which aspect of our psychology will win out? The needy, fearful self that sees itself as separate? Or the wise self that sees itself as part of a greater whole and wishes to coexist for the benefit of all? Which part of our nature do we choose to feed? Granted, we are inescapably tribal in nature. What makes the difference is if we see our tribe as closely held and constantly at odds with other tribes, or if we see the entire world as one great tribe.

The answer starts on a personal level. I believe the vast majority of people aspire to the same goals. They just get waylaid by the part of them that is fearful and will do whatever it can to survive. The first thing we need to do is see this fear clearly. How does it affect our behavior in ways big and small? Where does it come from?

BECOME THE LION

In *The Power of Now*, Eckhart Tolle states that fear is rooted in the ego. It is the part of us that is mind-based and concerned with the past and the future. It is separate and has no need for present moment experience. Its preoccupation with the past can manifest as guilt. Its concern for the future can manifest as anxiety or worry. Needless to say, this mindset is neither calm nor rational. Once you learn to observe your thoughts and emotions, they lose much of their illusory power. You become the lion.

Until then, your constant stream of thoughts is akin to a stranger walking into your home and following you around from room to room, jabbering constantly. You can't get away from him and have no control over what he will babble about next.

Close your eyes, try to be quiet for one minute, and think of nothing. Go ahead. Set a timer on your phone. I'll wait.

How was that? Did you notice thoughts coming out of nowhere and going in all directions without your conscious control? Here's an example of what that might have felt like:

> Set phone timer to 1 minute and go...
>
> *Okay, being quiet. Complete silence. (internal singing . . .) "Si-lent night, Ho-o-ly night. All is calm, all is bright." Is it round yon virgin or round young virgins? Man, Christmas is only four months away. (More singing . . .) "Away in a manger. No crib . . . "* MTV Cribs *was a cool show. That'd be nice to have a real theater and a pickleball court at my house. My house is a mess. I should reorganize my closet. Do I have clean underwear? I should do laundry. Oh yeah...quiet. Being quiet. I got this! (Stomach rumbles) Mmm . . . pizza. "Domino's Pizza delivers!" I haven't*

> *played dominos since I was a kid. I don't even remember how to play. I like those videos on the internet where some dude lines up all those dominos and . . .*

Alarm on phone goes off.

That's just a sample of what's going on when you're trying to be quiet. Imagine the noise taking place when you're on autopilot on a typical day.

Philosopher and best-selling author Sam Harris advocates seeing the mind as a tightly clenched fist. You look down and see that your hand has become a tight fist, squeezing hard. After a minute or so, the pain starts to become unbearable. Then you release it and the pain goes away. It is the same with the mind. You are angry, sad, or worried. "Why am I feeling like this?" You observe your mind and see that it is tightly clenched around a thought. You release the thought and the pain goes away. Sounds simple. So why do Buddy and his pals at the monastery spend lifetimes trying to get it right?

MEDITATION: LEARNING TO SEE AGAIN

The beginning of self-assessment is learning to observe your mind. Meditation can unlock this door. Watching thoughts come from nowhere, tumble around in all directions, and vanish into thin air is very instructive. When unobserved thoughts run your life and govern your actions, you give up control. Seeing what's rattling around in your brain might encourage you to stop and practice being the conductor rather than the passenger.

We are habitually lost in our heads. Discursive thinking is the state in which our minds incessantly jump from subject to subject.

Sometimes this process can produce solutions, but more often than not it's just a state of mind that is like a series of hamster wheels, spinning around but going nowhere. This is an example of living in your brain instead of your world. *On a deep level, not noticing your life is like giving it away.*

Have you ever been driving and suddenly realize that you don't remember anything at all about the last couple of miles? Learning to notice things and direct your own thoughts is a primary purpose of meditation. It's a pleasure and a relief to slow down the mind-babble and experience the present moment. When I find myself in a state of distraction, worry, or compulsive scenario-building, I try to remember to pause, take a conscious breath, and notice any tension in my body. As I release the tension and let my thoughts go, I allow space for noticing and am often fascinated by what I see.

Meditation is the training ground for this process but once you are acquainted with the technique, you don't need to always scurry around looking for the perfect spot under a tree to spend an hour in quiet tranquility. You can carve out brief interludes in the day to relax and simply notice what's happening around you and inside of you. A virtuous feedback cycle of noticing and gratitude can occur. I may have a headache but now notice that other parts of my body are pain-free and working beautifully. Maybe the dishwasher broke but I have running water. I look into the sky and really notice clouds for the first time in days, floating across a blue canopy, the sun peeking through and warming my skin. Rather than marinating in your own mental noise, consciously noticing your inner and outer world makes life richer and opens you up to ways of directing your mind toward gratitude and wonder.

THE SACRED PAUSE

The pickleball court is a perfectly acceptable venue for the practice of noticing. I wouldn't recommend sitting in the lotus position at the baseline and chanting between points (although that would be amusing—and time-consuming), but taking a moment to clear your mind and take a conscious breath is a good way to enhance focus and remind yourself why you're here. For some of us, the court is a refuge from other problems. We can relax and immerse ourselves in a game that lets us experience challenge without adding to the stress in our lives.

We don't have to be on watch 24/7, looking for potential trouble, and agitating about the friction of life. We have been given the unfathomable gift of consciousness. Nobody knows where it comes from, this awareness arising from a gathering of unconscious elements. So let someone else try to figure out why. In the meantime, enjoy every game. Wake up, give that mental hamster a break, and truly experience the life you have been given.

Tara Brach, in *Radical Acceptance*, calls this practice of stopping to observe thoughts the Sacred Pause: "When we pause, we don't know what will happen next. But by disrupting our habitual behaviors, we open to the possibility of new and creative ways of responding to our wants and fears."[1]

Meditation can have mystical aspects but at its heart it is highly practical. It's simply the process of pausing and noticing what's happening. There is power in the pause. Practice pausing before acting and see if your next action is more appropriate to the situation. A deep breath may facilitate this break in your mental stream. Creating this

[1] Tara Brach, *Radical Acceptance* (New York, NY: Penguin Life, 2019).

space will allow your higher self to engage with the world instead of the fearful ego.

Until we become conscious, all we are doing is acting out our conditioning.

One of life's greatest pleasures is the ability to respond from a conscious place when confronted with a difficult situation. Otherwise, we are like robots, predictably responding to stimuli. It is deeply satisfying to take control of your responses and be the person you want to be rather than the person you have habitually been.

OPENING YOUR PRESENCE

If you want to get the most out of your particular life circumstances, stay mindful that life is finite. We often live as if our days will never end, constantly looking ahead and worrying about an uncertain future or looking back at a past that has already been written. **Now is the time to live.**

The present moment is the only time and place that really exists. Meditation and the sacred pause offer gateways to this state of presence. So does immersion in art, conversation, or even pickleball.

There is joy and connection in the moment:

When you look into the eyes of your child or grandchild . . .

When you share a special moment with your spouse . . .

When you laugh with a friend . . .

When your dog snuggles up to you on the couch . . .

When you crack a winner down the line . . .

When you give unconditionally . . .

When you hear music that makes you move or brings you to tears . . .

When you feel the spark of discovery . . .

When you feel small but awed by the boundless sea or night sky . . .

This is bliss.

Learn to revel in these moments. In fact, learn to savor what may not seem extraordinary at all. If you look carefully enough, there are no ordinary moments. Widen your gaze, expand your sense of presence, and open yourself to every moment.

BABY STEPS AND SELF-COMPASSION

In *10% Happier*, Dan Harris makes a compelling case for improving your well-being but recommends a pragmatic approach that echoes what I suggest: Aim high but celebrate incremental progress. A 10 percent uptick in mindfulness, fitness, or emotional intelligence makes a noticeable difference. Just a few additional moments of awareness during your day can be mood-changing and life-altering.

Engage your mind to make specific, achievable change. Instead of trying to meditate for an hour every day and falling asleep at the twenty-minute mark (I have a "friend" that this sometimes happens to. His name is definitely not Mike.), start out by taking a deep breath and consciously pausing to give your brain time to make a decision with more clarity and less stress. Instead of embarking on a wholesale change to your diet, start by substituting lemon water for your morning beverage and celery with hummus for your afternoon snack. If you're about as flexible as a two-by-four, begin with gentle stretching instead of a one-hour yoga class. And don't jump on the pickleball challenge court before you learn the basic skills.

We are like any other machine. We require a "breaking in" period until we are able to operate at peak performance. We need proper fuel, maintenance, and down time to work at our best. We also need to realize that when we fall short of our goals, studies have shown that guilt and shame don't work. Self-compassion is the key to doing better next time. This is great news! Beating yourself up doesn't work and makes you feel like crap; you can officially be nice to yourself and get better results. Might as well start now. If you find that you are berating yourself when you make a mistake on or off the court, instead, imagine how you would talk to a child or a good friend when they make a mistake. Extend that same compassion and understanding to yourself.

THE TIME OF YOUR LIFE

> "The secret of life is enjoying the passage of time."
>
> –*James Taylor*

As you explore your game and your life, the role of time is essential to consider. On one level, your life travels on a long arc as you build your identity from childhood to old age. The optimal arc is based on long-term thinking and planning. But of course every life is comprised of moments.

The key is to live in awareness of the long and the short term simultaneously.

Without conscious direction, you flit from sensation to sensation, led around by unexamined emotions—sailing a boat without a rudder. However, if your eye is always cast toward the horizon, you miss the moments that make up the journey.

The book of your life is made up of many chapters; each chapter can be seen as a story in itself. Every job, relationship, and experience has a beginning and an end—the spark of discovery, the lifespan of the experience, and the inevitable rolling of the credits. Pickleball is one of those chapters for me. You may remember the first time you heard about the game or initially stepped on the court. In my case, I went for a run. I ended up running past the gym where I used to play basketball years ago. For old time's sake, I jogged in to look at the court and there were a bunch of folks playing on six courts with odd paddles and a plastic ball. They looked like they were having a good time and I asked one of them what they were doing. She said it was pickleball and told me to pick up one of the extra paddles in a box and give it a try.

That moment was the spark of discovery. But it was made possible by the long story of my life, which was based on an openness to ask questions, meet new people, and try new things. It was also made possible by maintaining good health and structuring my life to include free time so that I could take advantage of new opportunities. I am now somewhere on the spectrum of my pickleball life. I don't know how long this chapter will last and what will happen, but that's the fun of it. I never knew how many good people I would meet and how much I would enjoy the challenge of playing and improving; I certainly never thought I would write a book about it. And some day, injury, age, or some other factor will bring the chapter to a close.

This is how it is with everything in your life, from raising kids to your career to all of the seemingly random episodes that weave in and out of your time on this planet. But building the habits and awareness that prepare you to live a long and happy life will enable you to make the most out of every little story in which you play a part. And all of these stories, big and small, important and seemingly trivial, are made from moments.

Life seems to go on forever—until it doesn't. Repetition anesthetizes us to life's beauty and mystery. Sunrises, rainstorms and the ocean can lose their magic over us when we feel like we've seen the movie a thousand times before. We become lost in thought or rendered zombielike by our technological devices, losing touch with the miracle of nature and real human interaction.

Embracing life requires that we clear away the haze that envelops us over time. I am always awestruck when I travel to the mountains above Los Angeles and look down from the clear alpine air at the gray haze below that I mistook for sunshine when I was down in it. Return to the wonder of the moment and see the world as if for the first time. Whether you are on the court playing to eleven, or playing the long game of life, the moment is the only place you are alive right now. Your time is not limitless. Don't give it away, lost in negative emotional states, worrying about the future or stuck in the past. Savor the time you have been given; vividly notice and appreciate the sensation of being alive and conscious.

SPIRIT

"When you connect to the silence within you, that is when you can make sense of the disturbance going on around you."

– Stephen Richards

As you become more aware of how your body, mind, and heart should work together, you will come closer and closer to experiencing a life well lived. But what ties everything together is meaning and purpose: your spiritual nature.

Spirituality takes the process of living and gives it a greater context. It can be inextricably tied to a particular religion or it can be seen as a more secular pursuit that seeks to find meaning and connection without any affiliation. How you feed your spiritual self is up to you but I have found my connection through Buddhism. I am technically not Buddhist. There are tenets that I don't follow even though I respect them. (I promise I'll do the celibacy and no cheeseburger thing in my next lifetime. Honest.) And as with any spiritual concept that gets institutionalized, some people hijack the message for their own purposes.

Buddhism is a philosophy that offers insights as to how to live well that resonates with teachings from other religions. See if you agree with some of the following examples and find for yourself if they might help you live in better harmony with what is. "Ommmm . . ."

LESSONS FROM THE BUDDHA

Everyone suffers in one way or another. This is one of the core discoveries of the Buddha. He decided that his life's purpose was to reduce suffering wherever he found it. He came up with techniques to accomplish this and developed several key concepts to help light the way. You don't have to be a devout monk living in a cave to benefit from the teachings of Buddhism. Understanding a few core principles of this philosophy offers insights that make life easier. Buddhism is steeped in common sense that has lasted for centuries and maintains its relevance today. (Shaved head, orange robe, and chanting optional.)

Little Buddies in Laughing Buddha training.

THE MIDDLE WAY

Okay, I need to confess that this could actually be the title of this book. However, my idea of the middle way is a bit different than what Buddhism advocates. In the Western world, it can be impractical to live like a Buddhist monk. That's why I'm a big fan of Buddy, the Laughing Buddha. He gets me. I want to live with awareness and still be able to laugh and forgive myself when I screw up. Meditating for weeks on end and forgoing earthly pleasures would also put a crimp in one's business plan, not to mention happy hour. But there are still lessons that are relevant to our way of life.

The Middle Way advocates living between the extremes of hedonism and asceticism, pleasure and denial. At its best, life is savored in the present moment, neither caught up in desire nor shunning the joy of sensation and aliveness. Whether it is food, drink, sex, accumulation, or power, too much of a pleasure can warp a person and cause harm to themselves and others. Turning away from life to avoid the push and pull of desire can also be harmful. To paraphrase spiritual teacher Ram Dass: We are spirit, but while we're here, we might as well take the curriculum.

The concept of nirvana can be misunderstood to be ecstasy. More accurately, it means the cool state of mind in which desire is under control. When ego and desire lead us around by the nose, we can never be satisfied for long. There is always another thing, person, or experience that must be acquired. As Swami Mick Jaggernanda points out, one can't get no satisfaction. The state of nirvana is where you are neither compelled to grasp nor push away. It is flow. It is oneness. It is doing your best and accepting the outcome with equanimity. You love and give and you are imperfect and just fine.

SERENITY

> "Grant me the ability to change what I can, accept what I can't, and the wisdom to know the difference."
>
> – *Reinhold Niebuhr*

> "SERENITY NOW!"
>
> – *Frank Costanza (from Seinfeld)*

The Serenity Prayer is my favorite piece of advice for living a less stressful life. It doesn't come from Buddhism but it is congruent with the concept of acceptance. This prayer is such a simple template to apply to handle all situations. Of course, the wisdom is the tricky part. But looking at life's challenges from this perspective in a consistent, calm way will generate the required wisdom. It requires brutal honesty and discipline. When done properly, practicing this philosophy will reduce stress and guilt, provide clarity, and allow you to wisely embrace every challenge.

> "It is what it is."
>
> – *Everybody*

This is the modern corollary to the Serenity Prayer because it saves time and hardly anybody can remember the Serenity Prayer exactly...

("God grant me the wisdom to know what I can't, accept the difference, and change what I ... aw, hell ... It is what it is.")

On the court, serenity is a true asset. It promotes a relaxed mindset that leads to optimal decision-making. Acceptance keeps the game in perspective. Stressing out is not why we play the game. Pickleball is a refuge from more serious things. Sure, we all want to play our best. But when we fall short of perfection, *as we always do,* we need to check ourselves and reconnect with gratitude that we get to play a game at all.

When dealing with difficult people, you can try to change them or calmly point out that their actions are harmful. If they are not willing to change, the only wise course of action is to limit your contact with them. Remove yourself from the situation temporarily or permanently. This applies to random interactions and pickleball games, as well as to family, friends, and work dynamics.

When I am confronted with a difficult person and cannot change their behavior I sometimes try to develop instant compassion. I think, "How hard it must be to live like that. What has their life been like to make them behave this way? I only have to deal with this for a minute or two. What must it be like for those close to them to deal with this attitude constantly?" This mindset can sometimes defuse the other person whose negative energy needs more negative energy to feed itself. At the very least, nonreaction breaks the chain and allows you to return as soon as possible to your optimum state of mind.

In life, there are always situations that are not optimal. Your work, finances, and relationships are never perfect. Don't surrender before you consider all options to make effective change. But at that point you must accept what is beyond your control.

Another way to approach acceptance is to consider the concept of its opposite, resistance. Eckhart Tolle states that our degree of unhappiness can be simply measured as the amount of resistance to the present moment within us. This mental game has been very helpful to me when confronted with difficulties large and small. When a negative reaction to something starts to build in me, I try to stop and ask myself what I am resisting. As I ease my resistance I can literally feel my body relax. A deep breath usually accompanies this sensation and in mere moments I am able to act from a place of calmness and clarity.

See if you can play with this idea, find a way to recognize resistance, and get back to your regularly scheduled program airing *right now*.

COMPASSION

> "Compassion is your pain in my heart. Compassion is also your joy in my heart."
>
> – *Ken Druck*

As Ken points out, compassion isn't always directed toward pain. That is often the case, but it also can be a way to experience joy vicariously. In either case, the practice of compassion brings us closer to each other. It is the felt realization that we are all in this together. Everybody hurts but when we hurt together the pain becomes more tolerable. When we celebrate together at a rock concert, the positive energy vibrates through the crowd and lifts everyone, including the musicians, to greater heights. When we are compassionate, we reach out, take others into our heart, and create a kinship. We become each other.

Compassion is a funny thing. When we are compassionate toward others, they may not know or feel it, but we do. Of course, compassion that leads to action is best. In any event, genuine compassion benefits the giver. Even if compassion generates no change in an outcome, it creates kindness in ourselves and that kindness radiates from us in ways that enrich all with whom we come into contact. The next time you practice compassion, notice the feelings that arise in you. If it's warm and fuzzy, you're doing it right.

In *The Lost Art of Compassion*, Lorne Ladner describes the world we create through our emotions and compassion:

> "Emotions . . . serve as the motivating forces for how we humans transform the world around us. If we spend time dwelling on our desire, we gradually cocreate a world driven by greed, advertising, and compulsive consumerism. When we dwell in anger and fear, we cocreate a world filled with weapons, conflicts, and wars. To the extent that we dwell in love and compassion, we cocreate a world characterized by peace, mercy, safety, and inspiring beauty."[1]

That says it all.

MINDFULNESS

Mindfulness is the intelligent engine of change. It is a state of intense, peaceful noticing. Mindfulness is a place where you bring your higher self to the surface and tell your irrational, emotion-driven self to relax and take a seat. In my experience, this is the best you can be; acting instead of reacting—becoming intensely present so that you have a laser focus that is simultaneously calm and knowing.

---

[1] Lorne Ladner, "Conclusion: Vision and Embodiment," in *The Lost Art of Compassion: Discovering the Practice of Happiness in the Meeting of Buddhism and Psychology* (USA: Harper Collins, 2004), pp. 274-275.

Mind Full, or Mindful?

In relationships, this is a place where you see the other as yourself with lovingkindness and compassion. At work, you are engaged with your task, neither resisting nor distracted. In sports, this is "the zone," a place where the whole world disappears and it's just your mind and body as one entity in perfect flow. In any of these pursuits the goal is to visualize your actions and desires in harmony with your own personal nature as well as nature itself.

Mindfulness is as wondrous as it is difficult to achieve. There are so many distractions—so many emotions. The past and the future cry out for attention. Yet…

Here you are. Right now. Breath flowing, seeing, hearing. This is consciousness. This is who you really are when you peel away the layers. At some point, "you" disappear and consciousness is just manifesting itself through your presence. You are reborn into something far greater than your "self," without boundaries. (Man, I really need to lay off of those gummy bears when I'm writing.)

Anyway, mindfulness is the driver. When it takes the wheel, all those crazy parts of you come along for the ride. And good things happen.

AN IMPORTANT CAVEAT

So you now know more about what it takes to change your life for the better. It's going to be fun in many ways, but it will also take hard work and discipline. But what if you decide—in spite of all the evidence I've laid out that explains the physical, emotional, and psychological benefits of this journey—that it's not worth the trouble?

- "I just like to hit the ball around with my friends. I'm happy playing like I do."
- "I feel alive when I'm stressed."
- "I'd rather be fat and happy than thin and depressed."
- "I'd rather be lonely than miserable." (Or vice versa.)
- "I'm too far gone for any of this to matter. I'll just take life as it comes."

Fine.

Really. Perfectly fine.

Everyone gets to live their life as they see fit within certain constraints. Discipline can be difficult. As long as you realize what the path you are on looks like and are willing to live with the consequences, the decision not to change is a viable one. Maybe you'll beat the odds and outlive the woman next door who jogs by every day after her oatmeal-and-berries breakfast—and maybe you won't. Either way, it's your life and there are many ways to enjoy it.

You may also feel pretty good just as you are. You've gotten this far in life and pickleball and have done okay, thank you. Maybe you will be motivated to make a change or two here and there. That's great! If some small thing is useful to you within these pages, take it and move on. If not, no offense taken. There are a lot of ways to navigate this life. If you try to live well and not harm others, we are still on the same team.

However, with some new strategies, you can also decide to take on a new challenge and improve aspects of your life and game. You really can choose your life. At the very least, you can choose how to react to whatever comes your way from a place of awareness and power.

At the risk of saying it over and over again (because I'm not fond of beating a dead horse, or any horse. Really. Who would do that?), the prime directive is to find out what *your* enough is and at the end of the day to be okay with that. Life is a gift to you. Open it up and play with it. Try not to let it make you miserable because it's not exactly what you asked for, or what someone else thinks it should be. Throw out the old habits and ways of thinking that don't serve you. Enjoy the life that is you right now.

ACTION PLAN, PART 4

Write down what is causing you to suffer the most on a spiritual level. Are you caught reliving the past or worrying about the future? How can you find better balance in your life? Is there even a problem at all? Write down whatever comes up whether you feel a lack of connection, meaning, presence, or purpose. Now consider actual steps you might take and put them on paper (or virtual paper if you're on your computer). Maybe it's a meditation practice. If so, find a path, set out on it, and write down your experiences.

____

____

____

____

____

See if immersing yourself in the present moment changes the quality of your experience. Write down what you notice that may have slipped past you before. Write down what you are most grateful for and refer back to it often. Describe the sensations you feel when you are being actively compassionate. Research and write down the names of some books that might guide you on your spiritual quest. List people and activities that seem to feed your spiritual self.

____

____

____

____

____

THE BIG PICTURE

"Let me explain … No, there is too much. Let me sum up."
– Inigo Montoya (from The Princess Bride)

So …
I have made the case that playing our best and living our best lives are related journeys. Pickleball isn't as serious of an undertaking as skillfully navigating the ups and downs of life, but there are lessons to be learned from this interesting game that apply to the bigger picture.

- You lay the foundation for success by assessing where you are, then making a plan for improvement that is rational and enjoyable.
- You observe your mind and emotions to optimize your physical, strategic, and mental approach.
- You create new habits that enable you to reach your goals.

- You sharpen your abilities to embrace discipline and challenge and emerge with a profound gratitude that you get to play the game at all.
- You learn not to take yourself too seriously, appreciating the journey and accepting the results with equanimity and good will.

Let's finish by exploring some questions that tie things together. How do we deal with the unknown? How do we overcome obstacles that polarize our world? What gives life meaning? And how do we deal with the fact that every story has a beginning? And an end.

NOT KNOWING

There are many things we can know. Knowing brings comfort and enables us to move forward with solutions. However, in life, we often claim to know what is currently not knowable. People are willing to order their lives based on what others tell them is true without evidence, especially in our post-truth society where conspiracy theories sometimes have equal footing with reality.

It's hard to live without answers, especially when it comes to matters of suffering and death. I believe we should have faith and hope for the best, but remain humble as to what the real answers might be. The truth may be more incredible than we can imagine.

We also think we know more about the future than we do. We suffer from hindsight bias in that we overestimate our ability to predict past outcomes that could not possibly have been foreseen. This is the "I knew it all along" phenomenon. The result is we continue to confidently make predictions based on lack of information or misinformation.

By all means, seek answers, but understand that one of the most honest answers you can give is "I don't know." When the evidence is inconclusive and the outcome uncertain, admitting that you don't know is the first step to doing the best you can. I don't know what happens when I die but I can treat others well and let the chips fall where they may. There's no need to stress about outcomes. In fact, not knowing may be frustrating but it's why we wake up every day—we want to see what happens. We get to seek answers to the puzzle of life. Without mystery, life is just turning the pages of a book you've already read.

CAN I DO MORE?

Yes, you can always do more. It's worthwhile to maximize your abilities and achieve goals. But you can also become self-judgmental about not doing enough—guilt can creep in the side door. Eckhart Tolle offers great advice on this subject: once you decide to do something, give it your full attention and presence. It could be volunteering to feed the hungry at a local shelter. It could also be playing a pickleball game with your friends. Once the decision to do something is made, don't waste any time feeling guilty or resentful about the possible alternatives. Fully embrace your play time as much as your work time.

Examine if the need to do more is in alignment with your purpose or if it is a compulsion based on never feeling that you or your actions are enough. You can feel burned out or listless when living becomes a chore. Pause. See if you are living mindfully. If not, smile, let yourself off the hook without any guilt or blame, and get back in the game. Self-sustaining energy arises when you are living your best self in alignment with your purpose instead of trying to be everything to everyone.

HEROES

I strongly believe in emphasizing the positive but I'm not naive enough to see life as one big "pickleball kumbaya" where we raise our paddles to the sky transcending all borders, races, and religions as the sun shines down like a giant yellow pickleball of love on all of us. Life is hard. Nationalism, race, politics, and religion continue to be polarizing forces in spite of our common humanity. Forces beyond our control seek to tear us apart. Who or what will save us from ourselves?

Instead of another *Avengers* movie in which we face threats from afar like Thanos and rely on superheroes to save us, we are actually faced with threats of our own making: nuclear war, climate change, technological disruption, and polarization. We need a hero more than ever but unless Iron Man is living in your cul-de-sac and you don't know it, we need to save ourselves. What are our superpowers?

Like most tragic heroes, we want to do good but we are flawed. We get caught up in our ego, desire and fear. Rather than hardwiring happiness, we give in to our innate negativity, fixate on our separateness and fear "the other." When you are enough, you don't need to go to war with anyone to get more. You have what you need and can open yourself to others and compromise without undue fear.

Everyone wants to be happy but we tend to look at happiness as a zero-sum game; our happiness ebbs as someone else's rises. However, when we give freely of ourselves, our happiness doesn't diminish, it actually grows. The evolved mindset to which we should aspire is to give more, take less, and relax our grip on the paddle of life.

Good people can disagree about complicated things, but surely we can find ways to use our resources more wisely to ease the burden on our planet and the less fortunate. Those of us who have been winners in the "luck lottery" of life can share our good fortune without undermining our happiness. Remember that compassion is the felt realization that we are all in this together. Everybody hurts but when we hurt together and reach out to each other, our human connection grows and the pain becomes more tolerable. In my work with charities, I have seen the mutual uplifting of giver and receiver. You may be the hero to someone else today, but when hard times come your way, it's comforting to know there are kind souls ready to be the hero for you.

By now, I hope you have made the connection that skillful behaviors on the court and at the individual level extrapolate to our ability as a species to deal with the issues that threaten and divide us. I want you to get the most out of your game and live well, but I also want to add to the voices that are calling for a change in the way we see and interact with the world and others. It's up to each of us to be the hero the world needs right now.

THE CRUISE TO NOWHERE

I previously discussed perspective through the lens of pickleball pros who believe that keeping the game in perspective and playing with gratitude are the keys to enjoying your pickleball experience. The same lessons are evident wherever you go.

My wife and I recently spent a month floating at sea on a cruise ship, being refused entry to any port in our hemisphere as the 2020 pandemic exploded during our first week off the coast of Australia. We continued to zigzag the ocean looking for an escape. Eventually a blown engine convinced Hawaii to grudgingly allow us to disembark.

We got to observe up close and personal the many ways that people can respond to the same situation. From fist fights, insurrections, and imaginary drama on one side to kindness, acceptance, and gratitude on the other, passengers from all over the world showed their neuroses and their coping skills. Meanwhile the crew worked double-time to take care of their captive customers, smiling and serving while literally being spit on and berated at times. The crew had no idea when they would ever get home after all of us had disappeared down the gangway. They also faced the loss of their jobs as the cruise industry shut down. In spite of the luck of the draw that put them below deck, away from their families instead of in a balcony suite with an open bar, they showed the fortitude and attitude that often seem to escape the "lucky" ones.

I have spent time with multimillionaires who have everything—and nothing. I have sat and talked with those in Third World countries who have nothing—and everything. When your game or your life are getting you down, you know what to do. Check yourself. Count your blessings. Repeat as necessary.

PURPOSE

> "The heart of human excellence often begins to beat when you discover a pursuit that gives you a sense of meaning, joy, or passion."
>
> – *Terry Orlick*

What's your life's purpose? Anybody? Okay, I'll go first.

I'm with the Buddha on this one. He wrote, "All I teach is suffering and the end of suffering." My primary purpose is also to ease suffering wherever I find it. Whether it's inside of me, my friends, strangers, or the whole wide world, it's why I try to give more than I get. It's why I try to be the best version of myself so I can find peace and be available to help others. It's why I wrote this book.

If our purpose originates in kindness, we can build a world with less conflict rather than one with unnecessary struggle and acrimony. Your desires may be different. It might be to build a business, take care of your family, see the world, or create great art. Each of these is a viable goal but at the heart of any worthwhile pursuit is your own heart. What is the purpose that underlies these desires? Is it to explore and experience? Happiness? Self-actualization? Service to others?

There are many possible answers that define and guide our purpose. When I speak of easing suffering, my goal is to incorporate all of the above, happiness, exploration, self-actualization, and service. I try to keep these aspirations uppermost in my consciousness when I approach life from a bigger perspective. See if you can define your purpose in a way that imbues everything you are and do with its essence. Seek to leave a legacy that is a tribute to the fulfillment of your purpose.

YOUR ONLY TIME IS NOW

> "The unexamined life is not worth living."
>
> – *Socrates*

Take time to examine your life. When it nears the end, wouldn't it be nice to look back and see that it was a life well lived? Even the most famous of us will only be remembered for a short while before being reduced to footnotes in history. The rest of us will be almost completely forgotten in three or four generations at most. What can we learn from this?

You may not be remembered. But you will be experienced.

Your only time is now. There is a timelessness to your experience in both senses of the word. Your footprints will be erased by the tides of time. But the ripples of your actions and interactions will live on in the world you leave behind and in those who will follow.

It's fine to bounce around life, experiencing the ebb and flow of emotion and sensation, rarely diving deeper into the ocean of the mind and spirit. However, I hope I've shown that the interplay of emotion, rationality, and mindfulness is the fertile ground of the human experience—that each aspect feeds the other, providing a balance of sensation and contemplation. The more you engage your mind and live as a seeker, the more fulfilling your life can be. This engagement is at the heart of Socrates' bold words.

Life becomes more complicated when you dig deeper. It can be more comforting to not ask questions and rely on simple answers even when they are mere shadows of the truth. Yet when you confront that your searching yields no ultimate answer, but press on anyway, you are ennobled by the quest. It's the seeking that opens the door to purpose and meaning.

WHEN THINGS FALL APART

This is the title of a book by Pema Chödrön, an American Buddhist monk. Notice that the title is not *If Things Fall Apart*. Things are always falling apart. Earlier I discussed such important touchstones as acceptance and compassion. Now it is time to look at the concept of impermanence.

Life is like standing in an open meadow, painting watercolors as thunderstorms roll in. We rejoice in the "life-art" that emanates from us only to see it washed away by time and circumstance. Yet there is nobility in creation and perseverance in the face of certain impermanence.

Everything is impermanent. It's literally just a matter of time. One of those impermanent things is you. Not only will you die (I know, buzzkill) but everything and everyone around you will change and go away sooner or later. This is not breaking news. We know this, but we often don't act like we do. Our pickleball lives are subject to the same life cycle. We get injured, age, and someday we will dink our last. Until then, it's up to us to enjoy the gift of play while it is ours to savor.

The root of suffering is impermanence. We struggle to keep everything the same and hold on to what we have: relationships, status, our looks, our home, our stuff. When despite our best efforts, things break, people change, and we grow old, suffering happens. An understanding and acceptance of impermanence enables us to abide with what is true about our existence. When we give up our death grip on life, we allow ourselves to truly live.

This is not to say we should just give up on building the life we want since it's all going to fall apart eventually; we just don't freak out when things change. When we say that something went wrong, we often are just saying that something changed. When we live in harmony with impermanence we aren't as shocked when something falls apart. We can feel pain and grief depending on the magnitude of the event; this is a natural reaction. In the case of death, especially when it's unexpected or someone close to you, impermanence becomes more than a concept. It becomes hell.

In *The Real Rules of Life*, Ken Druck writes eloquently about the loss of a loved one. He says, "It never gets better. It gets different." He should know. When he lost his dear daughter, Jenna, at a young age in an accident, he was crushed beyond words—beyond pain. His healing still goes on to this day. The courage we use to face our fears is tested immeasurably more when our greatest fears become real.

His wounds will never completely mend but he has been able to rebuild his life by honoring her spirit rather than turning away and refusing to face the truth of impermanence. But it has taken time, and suffering. Yet today he shares images with me of his "Earth daughter," Steffi, and his twin grandsons. And his Jenna is still a part of his family, just separated by time and space.

The pain of being human is always with us. We grieve loss every day in ways ranging from having our car break down to losing those we treasure the most. Sometimes it's dealing with the little things that teach us to see the truth of impermanence. We feel sad and helpless, singled out to suffer by cruel fate. The reality is that nobody is singled out. It's simply life and loss in a dance of impermanence.

We can see the truth of our common experience with others when we expand our vision to the larger world. Nature is a great teacher in this regard. Because we don't relate as we do to fellow humans, the changes in nature are seen differently, even romanticized. The changing of the seasons and the circle of life can have positive connotations until we include ourselves in that circle and we experience our personal winter. Excluding ourselves from nature is an illusion. When we set ourselves apart from the true nature of reality, we rail against change and struggle to keep everything the same. In fact, life is always unfolding and evaporating simultaneously. Grieving is a natural reaction and a healing process that never ends, but eventually our suffering frees us to realize that impermanence is real and invites us to live in harmony with nature, never resisting, always changing.

THE QUIET POWER OF EQUANIMITY

Some of us are fortunate to be healthy, wealthy, and well loved, but many of us never hit that jackpot—and those who do can still be unhappy. Illness, financial problems, and relationship issues can make our days difficult. There is no sugarcoating that life can be hard; it certainly doesn't seem fair and it *will* fall apart. However, we have all observed people with problems who manage to keep a positive outlook and treat others well. They win at life because they develop an inner resolve to make the best of everything. I have seen the serene smile and kindness of cancer patients. I have traveled to places where financial wealth is not an option and seen those same people shift their emphasis to family and appreciating what little they do have. I have also seen those who do not have a functional family build their own family from scratch with friends, pets, and group affiliations like pickleball clubs.

This resolve is an affirmation of life itself. It is a spirit that refuses to let circumstances dictate attitude. When you live like this, you are as close to bulletproof as you can get. Tragedy and grief will still visit you but you will live the best you can in spite of what life throws at you.

FINAL WORD

As I said at the outset of our time together, pickleball can be seen as a metaphor for life. We approach both for the first time, unaware yet curious. We learn how to play, get along with others, and navigate the roadblocks to success. Along the way we learn lessons about ourselves and come to appreciate the challenge and the sense of belonging that make the game worth playing. In the end, we realize that when we try hard, have fun, and play nice, regret has no place in our hearts.

I want to thank you for coming along for the ride. Like any good road trip, I hope you remember the good times and forgive your driver for any wrong turns he might have made. My greatest wish for you is to live every day with passion and purpose, savoring all that life has to offer. May you face hard times with equanimity and compassion. May you play well, laugh often and feel the warmth of connection with others, and at the end of the day, look back with a smile on games well-played and a life well-lived.

YOUR PICKLEBALL POSTSCRIPT

NOW THAT EVERYBODY ELSE HAS shuffled away, contemplating deeper meanings and their place in the universe, it's just us. I noticed you fidgeting through all the serious stuff at the end but you kept it together and have been so patient and I'm very proud of you. I'll buy the beers next time we play.

You are no doubt so much more well-adjusted after reading this book, and are in a far better place to absorb the wisdom about to be bestowed upon you from the Pickleball Oracle. (If you are one of those people who skipped ahead to read this, you may be suffering from Pickleball Addiction Syndrome [PAS]. Before treating PAS with *Pickleball and the Art of Living*, consult your doctor or local pro. Side effects of reading this book may include Droopy Dinks, Third-Shot Flops, Cracked Balls and Kitchen Itch . . .)

So here it is—your guide to Pickleball Zen. Thanks for waiting . . .

THE ULTIMATE, COMPREHENSIVE PICKLEBALL GUIDE GUARANTEED TO ACHIEVE COMPLETE MASTERY AND DOMINATION, STRIKING FEAR IN THE HEARTS OF ALL WHO DARE CHALLENGE THE GREATNESS THAT IS YOU

Okay, maybe I oversold that a bit but the following section covers the basic strokes, core concepts, strategies and mental skills that can make you a complete player. My intent here is to hammer home the main concepts without going too deep. Sometimes too much information can be a bad thing; you can experience paralysis by analysis. It's good to do your research but when you're on the court it's better to keep just a few details front and center in your mind. As I sometimes remind myself and my students, "Dink, don't think."

There's no advice that perfectly applies to every skill level but there are general principles that serve as helpful guides. If you are a veteran pickler, some of this stuff may be obvious but it never hurts to be mindful of the basics. If you are new to pickleball, these observations may look like they are written in a foreign language, so feel free to skim this section until you start to get into the game.

THE STROKES

I won't get into specialties here like around-the-post shots and Ernes. That's better left for the post-grad pickleball book. Let's stick to the basics and a couple of tips for each stroke.

The Serve: For most players the serve is not a real weapon. The main focus should be accuracy and depth. Depth makes it more difficult for your opponent to get to the net. Get it in as deep as you can without making errors. Your serve probably won't win you a lot of points; just don't give away any freebies by hitting the ball out.

Return of Serve: Once again, depth is important. You want to put pressure on your opponent to make a difficult third shot. You also want to get all the way to the kitchen line to apply immediate pressure. If you find you're not getting all the way in, there's nothing wrong with hitting a high, arcing shot to give yourself time to get in position.

Third Shot: There's a reason the serving team is at a disadvantage in pickleball. The returning team gets to take up position at the kitchen line first. A good third shot is the equalizer. Without it, you get stuck deep in the court and it's usually just a matter of time until you lose the point. There are two choices for your third shot. In olden times (a couple of years ago,) a third-shot drop was the recommended play, dropping the ball softly over the net to force your opponent to hit a soft shot from below the net and allowing you to get up to the kitchen line without getting attacked. It's still the proper play for most skill levels but the influx of former tennis players and younger, more powerful hitters has seen the rise of the third-shot drive. The drive is an attempt to handcuff the opponent at the net by hitting a hard, flat groundstroke to entice an easy short ball return that can be hit hard or played softly more easily from further up in the court.

You need to be honest with yourself about your skill level and power capability. If you can't cause a weak return with your drives or you make too many errors, stick with the third-shot drop. I describe the third-shot drops to my students as "just a dink with a longer follow-through." Short-to-very-long is the mental image that works for me. Personally, I like to hit my third-shot drop to the backhand of the net player, usually the player in the ad court; this enables me to groove my shot and takes away any indecision about where to hit a shot that's already difficult enough. This is one topic about which players have different opinions. Listen to other perspectives and experiment to see what fits your game best.

Whatever you do, don't get caught admiring a good third shot from the baseline. The strategy is to hit a shot that allows you and your partner to move together toward the kitchen line and negate the positional advantage of your opponents.

Groundstrokes: If you play the game right, you shouldn't have to hit a lot of groundstrokes. Eighty to 90 percent of your shots after the third shot should be hit up at the kitchen line where you have a positional advantage. This ain't tennis; always try to work your way up to the net. When you do hit groundstrokes, use a short-to-long stroke and keep the ball low if your opponent is at the net.

Volleys: When a ball is below the net, a dink volley is the shot if your opponents are at the net. If your opponents are back in the court, I hit what I call a "rollover" shot, looping the ball over the net with moderate topspin to keep them back in the court and force them to hit another difficult shot. When the ball starts getting up around waist level, you have the option of hitting a soft volley low over the net or hitting firmly at or between your opponents to beat their reaction time. Higher balls should be volleyed hard at their feet, between them or into their body. If the feet are available as an option, that's usually the high percentage shot.

Overheads: The body mechanics for this shot are similar to tennis. You want to create rotation in your hips and shoulders to generate power. Unlike tennis, when you hit almost straight down on a pickleball, even when you smash it, it tends to pop up harmlessly. Overheads need to be hit at angles or deep in the court to be more effective.

Lobs: Used judiciously, the lob can turn around a point or catch your opponent off guard. Used injudiciously, a crappy lob might cause your partner to stare daggers at you when she takes an overhead off her butt as she turns around to avoid getting whacked in the face. Lobs are best used at the kitchen and directed over your opponents' backhands, where they can't get a powerful hit on the ball if it's a bit short. I avoid lobbing against young 6'5" guys with leaping ability. I am more likely to lob someone who is less mobile and more vertically challenged. Also, look for opportunities to lob when the wind is slightly against you as it gives you a greater margin for error than when you're downwind.

Dinks: I saved the best for last. The dink is the signature pickleball shot because the kitchen line keeps players seven feet from the net on balls hit in the air. You need to mix in short, soft dinks to move your opponents around and keep them from attacking you. It's the main reason why pickleball is a mix of finesse and power. This puts a premium on thinking your way around the court, mixing up shots, and strategizing on how to construct points. In my opinion this is what makes pickleball so addictive and inclusive. You don't necessarily have to be an amazing athlete. (Okay, it helps.) You learn to use guile and finesse to set up opportunities.

The dink itself demands a very short-to-long stroke with the paddle presented out in front of you. The stroke promotes accuracy and the paddle position allows you to contact the ball earlier and decrease your opponents' reaction time. The strategy is to move your opponents around and hit at their feet whenever possible to induce a pop-up that you can attack. It's often a game of cat and mouse that can last many strokes. It's a test of patience, skill, and strategy. Expert dinkers can put their opponents on a string and control points. Good dinking makes the rest of your game immeasurably better.

GENERAL PRINCIPLES AND STRATEGIES

It's one thing to learn the proper strokes. It's another thing entirely to play intelligently, consistently executing optimal strategies to get the most out of your game. Here are some concepts that can take ordinary athletic ability and turn it into extraordinary results.

Keep the Ball Low: High balls get crushed or go out.

Respect the Net: Even though the ball must be kept low, I have completed a rigorous statistical analysis and determined that roughly 100 percent of the balls that don't clear the net result in lost points. Dinks and third-shot drops should reach their apex on *your* side of the net with sufficient clearance to reduce errors.

Compact Strokes/Short-to-Long: A short-to-long stroke promotes acceleration through the ball and invites cleaner contact. The longer the backswing, the more bad things can happen before contact is made. A long swing also telegraphs your intentions.

The Middle Way: Not only a practical Buddhist concept, the middle of the court is the most practical area to direct your shots. Not only is the net 2" lower in the center than at the sidelines, confusion is caused by hitting a ball between your opponents. Hitting to the middle also allows you to …

Reduce Unforced Errors: Hitting winners is sexier but keeping the ball in the court, and your opponents off-balance, will result in higher percentage putaway winners when the time is right. Don't try "hero shots" when a higher percentage shot is the proper play. Set up your points.

Hit Low Balls Soft and High Balls Hard: Don't try to hit winners from ankle level. And when you do all the hard work to induce a shot that you can be aggressive with, take the shot!

Hit at the Feet: Is it hard for you to hit a ball directed at your feet? Yes, it is. So why not give your opponent the pleasure of this experience? Some days I make a game out of focusing on hitting to my opponent's feet wherever they are on the court. Those days usually go well for me.

Get to the Kitchen Line (and Don't Retreat!): If you aren't at the kitchen line, every shot you hit should be designed to get you there ASAP. Once there, don't move back to hit a shot and then stand there. When you do this you expose your feet and you know what we do when we see a juicy pair of sneakers. We hit them with a little yellow ball.

Move Your Feet: But not too much. Get into proper position every time with quick, precise footwork. A common mistake I see with lower level players is leaning for a shot instead of taking a couple of quick steps to get in optimal position. Just don't get happy feet and move around unnecessarily, getting yourself out of position, especially at the kitchen line.

Weight Steady or Forward: Moving backward while hitting forward is asking for trouble. Use those things at the end of your legs (feet) to get behind the ball and execute your shot with your weight steady or slightly forward.

Stay Well Behind the Baseline on the Return of Serve: This habit keeps you from moving backward as you hit, which we just discussed. Moving backward stops you from getting to the kitchen line quickly as well. If your opponent doesn't hit hard serves, then adjust your position forward in the court.

Don't Wander into the Court after You Serve: Continuing a theme here. If you move into the court a couple of steps after serving, you expose your feet and a good opponent will attack that spot causing you to move backward and hit an awkward shot.

Talk: Not between points, during them. Give a firm "yours" or "mine" call on balls down the middle. Make the same call on lobs hit over your heads. When you hit a third-shot drop, verbally let your partner know you've hit a good one and are charging in by saying "go" or something to that effect. If you hit a bad one, you can say "uh-oh," "stay," or "oh, s&%#." They'll get the message.

Placement Over Power: Learning to place the ball where your opponent can't use power against you is key. And placing the ball in the right spot can force a weak shot, setting you up to use *your* power game.

Be Quick but Don't Hurry: This is advice from John Wooden, the legendary UCLA basketball coach. Get to the ball or the proper position on the court with as much quickness as you can muster, then relax and don't hurry your shot. Stop and execute a split-step before you hit as you make your way from the baseline to the kitchen. Only then do you continue on to the kitchen line. Never be moving when your opponent is about to strike the ball unless you are properly anticipating a shot that will cause you to cover some ground.

Court Positioning: Your position on the court directly affects your results in the game. The prime directive is to get to the kitchen line but there are other tips that tilt the odds in your favor. Move together with your partner to the net to avoid leaving your opponents easy options and gaps to exploit. In the dink game, shift position to help your partner when he's pulled wide. When at the net against bangers in the backcourt, shift your position toward the side of the hitter to take away the line and middle options. If they can hit a hard crosscourt winner from deep in the court, applaud politely. In general, pinch the middle as that is where most smart players (like you) are hitting high percentage shots.

Make Your Shots Look the Same until the Last Moment: The element of surprise takes away reaction time from your opponent, especially at the net. Practice executing dinks, snaps (quick flicks at the opponent's body at the kitchen), and lobs with the same preparation to keep 'em guessing.

Have a Plan for Shot Selection: Keep the ball low or hit it hard as the situation dictates. Don't panic and hit what I call a middle shot that floats up around chest level and politely asks to be crushed. This is why you have to put in the work to make your shot selection intuitive. Sometimes you're forced into an error but try to never hit a ball that sits up because you are undecided.

Good players master these fundamentals. Their consistent technique, shot selection, and strategy reduce unforced errors and grind down their opponents. Their opponents might think that they are playing poorly when they are actually being consciously forced into difficult situations by the application of core concepts and superior strategy.

THE MENTAL GAME

Another way to get the edge on your opponents and enjoy the game more is working on your mental game. We can be our own worst enemies on the court when our mental game sabotages our physical game. Here are some keys to help you get out of your own way, play mentally strong, and not let the occasional bad game ruin your day.

Study Your Opponents: Don't just play your regular game against everyone. If they don't move well, mix in some drop shots and lobs. If they really favor their backhand when dinking, test their forehand. If they seem to get flustered with balls hit hard right at them, it may be time to go at them and play the "raise your hand apologetically and say 'sorry' (not really sorry)" game.

The Comparison Trap (Pickleball Version): You will dominate at some skill levels and get crushed at others. That's why there's a rating system in pickleball. In general, you want to play with people at or slightly above your level if you want to enjoy the game and continue to improve. This isn't always possible. If you find yourself in a game below your skill level, practice with a purpose, work on certain shots, and encourage your partner and opponents. When you find yourself above your skill level, stay positive, and resolve to play your game regardless of the outcome. Limit your errors and don't get caught up in the score or apologizing after every point.

Some friendly advice that you probably don't need but must be said: don't look to get into games that are way above your skill level. It's no fun for you, and believe me, it's no fun for them either. If an advanced group needs a fourth and invites you in, be your wonderful self-deprecating self, let them know they're probably a bit above your pay grade but you're happy to play if it helps them pull a game together. When you do this, it takes the pressure off of you and encourages them to be helpful and considerate since they know what they're getting into.

Know Thyself: We all bring different skill sets and mental acumen to the court. If you have already established a "kinetic chain" that enables you to blend your movements into a natural hitting motion you will have a much easier time picking up and internalizing skills. However, some of us have to build a game from the ground up, learning proper body positions and sequences step by step. It's essential to understand where you are on this spectrum. Only then can you work toward realistic goals with the right attitude rather than experiencing discontent because you can't do what the more advanced players seem to do effortlessly.

Stay Relentlessly Positive: When you miss shots, it's not a reflection of your self-worth. It might be a sign that you need to practice a certain aspect of your game. It's also possible that your opponent just executed a good shot. Either way, put it aside and play the next point as well as you can. Self-criticism is a poor substitute for calmly analyzing and learning from your mistakes. WE ALL MISS! Sometimes you do everything right and you just flat-out miss the shot. Laugh it off; you'll make the next one.

Don't Take It Personally: We are so blessed to be able to play this game ... any game for that matter. If you are playing with or against a player who upsets you in any way, realize that you don't have to spend the rest of your life with them, just the next fifteen minutes or so. Make the best of it and then find another game.

The same mindset applies if your teammate doesn't play as intelligently as you do. You brilliantly work your way to the net with a deft combination of drops and volleys only to find that your partner is out of position, hitting low percentage shots, and allowing your opponents to give you a nice assortment of pickleball tattoos. You can offer constructive advice, but sometimes the only thing you can do is thank them for the game, rub your bruises, and move on to greener pastures. This is another reason why it's important to find the right game with people at your level.

Balance: Mental toughness and psychological assets do you little good if you are not executing the physical fundamentals properly. Physical ability is limited by poor shot selection, low percentage play, and a mind that is cluttered by unhealthy attitudes and mental noise. The goal is to bring your body, mind, and emotional state into alignment to produce the best pickleball and life experience possible.

PUTTING IT ALL TOGETHER

The perfect pickleball cocktail is one part technical, one part strategic, and one part psychological ... with a garnish of gratitude. The technical part is grooving your strokes through diligent practice and game situations, mindfully moving and positioning yourself on the court. The strategic part is implementing proper, high percentage shot selection, reducing errors, and using your strengths to exploit your opponents' weaknesses. The psychological part is playing with realistic expectations, avoiding self-judgment, and enjoying the game and your friends.

When your game is firing on all cylinders, you will play your best and enjoy it more. People want to play with and be with players who try hard, play smart, and are positive. It's just a plastic ball. Do your best and enjoy every day you get to play.

Lessons and drills

Lessons and drills are the homework of your pickleball education. Improvement isn't a passive process; it requires action to make it a reality. I'm always trying to pick up and share information with others to improve our games. Find someone who shares your passion for learning and work together to develop new shots, work on any weaknesses, and sharpen your skills. Lessons are imperative for beginners. So much time is wasted grooving the wrong patterns when there is plenty of instruction available.

DEAR DIARY...

I keep a pickleball journal and I encourage my students to do the same. It's been proven that writing things down is the best way to commit information to memory so it's helpful to have a resource handy with the best tips you've picked up over the years that you might otherwise forget. If you want your game plan to have staying power, check back in on the fundamentals occasionally. See which parts of the plan are producing results and tweak the parts that don't seem to be working as well.

It's also fun to include stories and pictures in your journal if you want to look back fondly on when you were young and beautiful like the gentlemen in the picture below.

I taught those guys to the left everything they know.

I hope the preceding section provides a good foundation for your pickleball journal. Embrace the challenge to unlock the best game that lies within you, but above all, have fun. That's a sure sign you're on the right track.

Now get out there and dominate those bums who think they can hang with you! Crush them! Show no mercy! (Sorry, that was uncalled for. What I meant was, "Play in the present moment, treasuring your relationships and valuing the journey above results." Geez, this enlightenment stuff is hard ...)

"Cliff Notes"

The goal of this journey is to fine-tune your mindset to get the most out of your game and your life—and have fun along the way.

A day well lived or a game well played is one in which you have consciously given the best version of yourself, no matter what that is.

We are not rational beings. We are rationalizing beings.

A life well lived is a celebration of who you are. It is not belittling yourself on some level for who you are not.

Feel the difference between mindlessly feeding a desire and living well.

Try hard. Have fun. Play nice.

Until we become conscious, all we are doing is acting out our conditioning.

Eat well. Keep moving.

The quest to be better is not a condemnation of who you are—it is an opportunity to find new versions of yourself that may be even more satisfying and fulfilling.

What you learn will reshape your life.

The goal is not mastery to the point of misery.

Mindfulness, long-term thinking, and perseverance is what will set you apart in a short attention span world.

You may not be remembered. But you will be experienced.

THE ROAD MAP

- *Assess Yourself*
- *Understand the Interplay of Mind and Emotion*
- *Develop a Growth Mindset*
- *Engage Your Higher Self*
- *Create "Success Environments"*
- *Develop Perspective and Self-Compassion*
- *Live in the Present Moment*

PICKLEBALL INSTRUCTION RESOURCES

Steve Dawson
Bobby Riggs Racket & Paddle
Encinitas, California
bobbyriggs.net

Morgan Evans
CoachME Pickleball
coachmepickleball.com
Podcast: Pickleball.FM

Mark Renneson
Third Shot Sports
thirdshotsports.com

Irina Tereschenko
Instagram: @sicktrx_irina

Appendix

RADICAL ACCEPTANCE: Embracing Your Life with the Heart of a Buddha

– Tara Brach

WHEN THINGS FALL APART: Heart Advice for Difficult Times

– Pema Chodron

8 MINUTE MEDITATION: Quiet Your Mind. Change Your Life.

– Victor Davich

THE REAL RULES OF LIFE: Balancing Life's Terms with Your Own

– Ken Druck, PhD

MINDSET: The New Psychology of Success

– Carol Dweck

MY STROKE OF INSIGHT: A Brain Scientist's Personal Journey

– Jill Bolte Taylor, Ph.D.

OUTLIERS: The Story of Success

– Malcolm Gladwell

HARDWIRING HAPPINESS

– Dr. Rick Hanson

HOMO DEUS: A Brief History of Tomorrow

– Yuval Noah Harari

10% HAPPIER: How I Tamed the Voice in My Head, Reduced Stress without Losing My Edge, and Found Self-Help That Actually Works—A True Story

– Dan Harris

THE RHYTHM OF LIFE: Living Every Day with Passion & Purpose

– Matthew Kelly

THE LOST ART OF COMPASSION: Discovering the Practice of Happiness in the Meeting of Buddhism and Psychology

– Lorne Ladner

UNDO IT!: How Simple Lifestyle Changes Can Reverse Most Chronic Diseases

– Dean Ornish, M.D., and Anne Ornish

THE FOUR AGREEMENTS: A Practical Guide to Personal Freedom

– Don Miguel Ruiz

THE UNTETHERED SOUL: The Journey Beyond Yourself

– Michael A. Singer

THE POWER OF NOW: A Guide to Spiritual Enlightenment

– Eckhart Tolle

Acknowledgments

Acknowledgment is a nice word but it doesn't seem sufficient to express my gratitude to the following special people. First, to my wife, Diane: life partner, fellow traveler and love of my life—I'm so proud to be one of your two favorite husbands ever. To my parents, Bill and Lolly: thanks for all the free food and rent growing up. But seriously, thanks for absolutely everything; I cannot imagine a better Mom and Dad. To my kids and kid-in-law, Sarah, Nick and Alec, you're amazing—The Lemon of Truth knows this to be so. To Rowan: stop being such a baby and get a job.

To Ken Druck, for the swift kick in the arse to start writing and all of your great advice. To Sara Stratton at Redwood Publishing, for your kindness and guidance. To Karla, for a nudge in the right direction. To Blanche, my favorite teacher ever. To my friends: for the laughter and the trust. To those in the pickleball community who have contributed to this book and filled my days with competition and camaraderie, a grateful paddle tap to you all.

Interior Image Credits

David Leonett: 2-3; Henck van Bilsen: 146; Mike Branon Personal Collection: 10, 11, 66, 106, 176, 187; Patrick Kelley: 38, 68; Photographer Unknown: 22; pickleballteezers.com: Redwood Publishing, LLC, 31; 37; Shutterstock Animal Footprint/Hanna Tsy (stock vector ID: 320989325): 21, 61, 84, 109, 122, 133, 145, 161; Shutterstock Attention Sign with Exclamation Mark Symbol/NEGOVURA (stock vector ID: 154829042): 21; Shutterstock Bodybuilder Flexing His Muscles in Studio/Istvan Csak (stock photo ID: 92543452): 71; Shutterstock Detour Sign/alexmillos (stock illustration ID: 120225865): 41; Shutterstock Diet Change Healthy Lifestyle Concept/Lightspring (stock photo ID: 277748333): 65; Shutterstock Novice Three Seats on the Timber and Laughing/Ninja SS (stock photo ID: 405715642): 140; Shutterstock Smiling Buddha Statue/Dostoevsky (stock photo ID: 49499209): 8; Shutterstock Veggies: 65; Shutterstock Weak Young Man Muscle Flexing Isolated on the White Background/Sabphoto (stock photo ID: 58130732871; Total Mind Power Institute: 22.

Chapter start vector image: freepik.com

A percentage of the proceeds from the sales of this book will be donated to charities for disaster and hunger relief.

If you enjoyed the book, please spread the word or leave a review on Amazon. “Word of mouth” (or word of internet?) means a lot. Feel free to visit mikebranon.com for blogs, updates and features to improve your game, health, and well-being. Thanks!

-Mike